BIRMINGHAM AT WAR

ALTON DOUGLAS

GORDON STRETCH

CLIVE HARDY
ADDITIONAL RESEARCH BY JO DOUGLAS

BIRMINGHAM AT WAR

© 1982 ALTON DOUGLAS, GORDON STRETCH, CLIVE HARDY AND JO DOUGLAS
© 1994 ALTON AND JO DOUGLAS
Published by Brewin Books, Doric House, Church Street, Studley, Warks. B80 7LG.
Printed by Heron Press
12th Impression March 1997
ISBN No. 0 947731 93 8

c/o Brewin Books
Doric House, Church Street,
Studley, Warks B80 7LG.

Dear Nostalgic,

Like you, I'd often thought there ought to be, in book form, a pictorial account of events in Second World War Birmingham. I'd scoured the library shelves until my brown borrower's tickets fell into disuse and were replaced by a variation on the credit card theme, and all in vain. So, in the hope that this would please both you and me, my friends Gordon Stretch and Clive Hardy, my wife Jo, and yours truly, produced the labour of love you hold in your hands now.

My interest was stimulated at an early age, because my father was Deputy Head A.R.P. Warden for Small Heath, my brother was in the Home Guard, Mum eternally aproned and headscarfed was really Everyman's Mum, and I, wearing a Mickey Mouse gas mask (remember those?) and siren suit, and armed with a tin machine gun, crouched under the stairs at 290, Heather Road, Small Heath, personally brought down more German planes than anyone else in the whole wide world.

I found, during the period of researching this book, as I criss-crossed hundreds of miles backwards and forwards across our city, sometimes finding a nugget of gold and now and then just a splinter that, even without realising it, the sounds I chose to listen to were those of the Swing Era — Miller, Dorsey, Goodman, Shaw and so on. My thoughts, as I travelled the streets, were of marching men and women, devastation, mugs of tea, comradeship, heroism and above all were of wonderment that the human spirit could survive and triumph over anything (even some of those mugs of tea).

As I visited homes, in search of that elusive photograph, people poured out not only the contents of their attics, but also their hearts too, and for that I'll be eternally grateful.

I hope you'll forgive any minor errors. After 40 years some facts are hard to pin down, memories are not always as one with reality — and some of us even have difficulty remembering what colour socks we're wearing. Also the number of excellent photographs which had to be omitted, due to lack of space, was quite heartrending.

Anyway this is a book especially for you to dip into. Use a magnifying glass on some of the pictures and you'll be amazed at the treasure that is yours for the finding. Above all, of course, say a silent "Thank You" to the people of the forties who made it possible for us to enjoy the eighties.

Yours, in friendship,

3

CONTENTS

Page

THE ROAD TO WAR

"This is not peace, it is an armistice for twenty years." These prophetic words were spoken by the French Marshal Foch at Versailles on 28th June 1919. On that day Germany signed what was by far the most important of the five treaties which together made up the Peace of Paris.

Under the terms of the Treaty of Versailles, Germany was virtually disarmed. Her army was limited to 100,000 men, her once proud High Seas Fleet reduced to little more than a coastal defence force, and her air force disbanded. The east bank of the Rhine was to be demilitarised to a depth of 50 miles and her colonies taken away. The provinces of Alsace and Lorraine were ceded to France (though the French had wanted the entire west bank of the Rhine), Malmedy and Eupen went to Belgium, the West Prussia and Posen were incorporated into the newly independent state of Poland. The ports of Memel and Danzig together with the Saar were placed under allied occupation, through Danzig later became a free state. All occupation costs were to be borne by Germany. Article 231, the War Guilt Clause, was by far the most important. Germany was forced to accept "responsibility. . .for causing all the loss and damage. . .as a consequence of the war imposed. . .by the aggression of Germany and her allies." Germany was to pay reparations to the allies of around £2,000 million at 1919 prices.

In March 1930 the Weimar Republic had embarked on a series of deflationary policies in an attempt to free Germany from paying reparations. One of those policies was to keep unemployment artificially high. The scheme in effect backfired. Out of the misery caused by unemployment (6,000,000 by 1932 and rising) and low pay for those fortunate enough to have work grew the class, ideological and racial hatreds upon which the National Socialist Party fed. In 1928 there were only 12 National Socialist deputies in the Reichstag. By 1930 the number had grown to 107.

Adolf Hitler would never have come to power, as he did in January 1933, had it not been for the depression. He was a blend of shrewd politician and opportunist, and he had set his sights on dragging Germany out of her economic doldrums and re-establishing her as the leading European power. That he achieved his aims within six years is testimony to both his political skill and his fanaticism.

Hitler had long dreamed of incorporating his native Austria into the Reich, and by the beginning of 1938 he was ready to move. On 12th February, the Austrian Chancellor Schuschnigg met Hitler at Berchtesgaden and agreed to include Austrian Nazis in his government. The question of incorporating Austria into the Reich was raised, but no formal agreement reached. Hitler received a shock several weeks later when Schuschnigg decided that a plebiscite would have to be conducted. Fearing that the result might go against unification, the German High Command improvised invasion plans during the night 9th/10th March. Austria was annexed two days later. France, the only landpower in the west,

had no military plans to aid Austria and in any case was without a government on 12th March. On 13th March Hitler entered Vienna.

On 5th November 1937, Hitler met in secret session with his military advisers. Alas a complete record of this meeting no longer survives, the only extant information being the Hossbach Memorandum drawn up by Hitler's adjutant, Colonel Hossbach. However, it gives some idea of what Hitler was thinking. If Germany failed to complete military operations by 1945, at the latest, not only would the economic pressures be too great to bear, but her armed forces would find themselves with a high proportion of obsolete weapons. Hitler, ever the opportunist, saw two possible avenues for German expansion in central Europe — firstly the crippling of France by civil war, secondly picking up the pieces following an Anglo-French-Italian war arising out of Mediterranean tension. Indeed one of the reasons why France had failed to act in the Rhineland was because she had transferred 14 divisions to the Alps and Tunisia due to the Abyssinian crisis. The Hossbach Memorandum contained indications of Hitler's more immediate plans, namely the seizure of Austria and Czechoslovakia.

Czechoslovakia came into being in 1918 and had the makings of a flourishing economy, but there were problems. Her population of 13.5 million was made up of 8.5 million Czechs and Slovaks, 3.75 million Germans, 1 million Magyars and minorities of Poles, Ruthenes and Jews. With such a diverse population, relations between the different nationalities were strained, yet despite this Czechoslovakia prospered. By 1925 she was one of only three nations involved in the war that had surpassed their 1913 levels of manufacture. The Wall Street crash in October 1929 had a devastating effect on her industries. With countries abandoning the gold standard and introducing import tariffs, the demand for Czech goods fell. The major industrial area suffered from high unemployment, in particular the predominantly German-populated Sudetenland. The continuing depression bought support for the Sudeten Nazi Party which, led by Konrad Henlein, won 44 seats in the 1935 elections.

Many, including Neville Chamberlain, believed that Hitler would strike again and that Czechoslovakia was his target. Until the winter of 1937-8, German military planning had been purely defensive, although on 27th June 1937 a general directive provided for two possible deployments. Plan Red was to defeat a major French invasion in the west whilst holding a defensive line against possible Czech/Polish intervention in the east. Plan Green called for a pre-emptive strike against Czechoslovakia whilst holding a defensive line against possible French intervention in the west. On 7th December 1937 Plan Green was given priority. Germany was now moving onto a war footing. On 20th February 1938, Hitler gave a speech in which he promised protection to Germans living outside the Reich, a speech which the Sudeten Nazis seized upon to further their own cause with a campaign for separation that

PICTURE 4

Anti-gas fire-fighters in Victoria Square for the parade of Auxiliary Fire Service Members, March 1938.

continued throughout the summer.

By March 1938, Anglo-French policy on the Czechs was both ill-informed and unsympathetic. The British Cabinet decided that Czechoslovakia was indefensible — without consulting the French or awaiting military advice. On 24th March, Chamberlain told the House of Commons that he refused to widen Britain's commitments under the Treaty of Locarno to include intervention in a Franco-German war arising out of the French going to the aid of Czechoslovakia. In any case Chamberlain saw no benefit to Britain in a free Czechoslovakia. Indeed, he shared Hitler's dislike of her alliances with France and the Soviet Union. Another influence upon Chamberlain was the attitude of the Dominions, who had little or no sympathy for a British guarantee to the Czechs. Chamberlain believed that by extracting concessions from the Czech government that would satisfy both Hitler and the Sudeten Germans, then a general European war might be averted, and valuable time could be bought, for the longer Britain had to rearm, the greater her chances of victory, especially if she had to fight alone.

An interesting point here is that Hitler too was trying to avoid a general war. Though Germany's pre-1939 military build up had been greater than that of Britain, France and the United States, it took until 1942 for her to achieve a total war economy. In 1939 the German army comprised 51 divisions, but with only 6 weeks' supply of munitions. It appears that Hitler was planning a series of short wars against Czechoslovakia in 1938, Poland in 1939 and Russia in 1941. The last thing Hitler wanted was a war of attrition against Britain and France.

May saw a crisis point in the Czechoslovakian question. With Czechoslovakian municipal elections to be held on 22nd May, Konrad Henlein, acting upon orders from Berlin, visited London on 12th to 14th May. Henlein, convinced that the British government was sympathetic, reported back to Hitler. Within 4 days, Europe was gripped with the news of German troop movements and a partial mobilisation of Czech forces. With 35 divisions, including some of the best armour of the period, the Czech army would certainly have given a good account of itself. However, the Czech government could not act without French, Soviet or British support,

PICTURE 5

Barrage balloon demonstration in Aston Park, March 1939.

none of which was forthcoming. Instead of offering military assistance the British and French went in for political arm bending, telling the Czechs to give in to Hitler's demands on the Sudetenland.

On 4th September the Czech President, fearing civil war, agreed to all the demands made by the Sudeten Germans. On the 13th Hitler demanded self-determination for the Sudetens. The following day rioting broke out, Martial Law was declared and Henlein fled to Germany. Hitler, taking a gamble that Britain and France would not get involved militarily, met Chamberlain and Sir Horace Wilson at Berchtesgaden and demanded the annexation of the Sudetenland. On the 18th, Daladier came to London and it was agreed that those areas in which more than half the population were German should be ceded to the Reich. With Hitler setting 1st October as a deadline beyond which military options would be used, Chamberlain again met the Fuehrer. Sensing victory, Hitler upped the price of peace to include the handover of all military installations intact and a plebiscite in all other areas with

German minorities. Since this would have resulted in Czechoslovakia handing over even more territory, Chamberlain stood his ground. On the 23rd Czechoslovakia mobilised. With Britain pledging her support for France in the event of a German attack on Czechoslovakia Hitler had lost his chance to launch his pre-emptive strike and a conference was hurriedly arranged.

On 29th September the Munich Conference was convened, though neither Czechoslovakia nor the Soviet Union were represented. The result was a foregone conclusion. Signed in the early hours of the 30th, the agreement provided for the German occupation of the Sudetenland in 10 days from 1st October.

Chamberlain's personal achievement at Munich was the Anglo-German Declaration of the 30th. Without saying anything to the French, Chamberlain and Hitler met in private and signed a statement to the effect that the two countries would never go to war again — "peace in our time."

What would have happened if Germany had invaded Czechoslovakia in 1938 is open to

PICTURE 6

2/7th Batt. Royal Warks. (Territorial) marching into camp at Arundel, 6th August 1939.

PICTURE 7
The Warwickshire Yeomanry riding along Bristol Street towards the Horse Fair, May 1939.

speculation. Militarily the French could meet the Germans on at least even terms. The Germans were short of munitions, fuel and trained reserves and the bulk of the army was deployed against Czechoslovakia leaving only 10 divisions in the west facing the French.

The German occupation of the Czech provinces of Bohemia-Moravia on the 15th/16th March 1939 and the annexation of Memel five days later finally convinced the Western powers that in future they would have to act more firmly. On 24th March, Britain and France agreed to resist any German aggression against Holland, Belgium or Switzerland. One week later Britain said that she would stand by France in guaranteeing Poland's frontiers. On 3rd and 11th April, Hitler issued directives to prepare for an attack on Poland.

With a population of 27 million, Poland's affairs were dominated by her relations with her neighbours, none of whom were too pleased with the frontiers settled on her by the Treaty of Versailles. With such hostile neighbours, Poland sought security in an alliance with France in 1921 and later one with Roumania. A non-aggression pact was signed with the Soviet Union in 1932, but the real threat came from Germany, especially so after the Nazi Party had gained control of Danzig. Hitler, probably inspired by the fact that Britain and France had done nothing militarily to stop him in Czechoslovakia and Austria, decided that the time had come to settle the Danzig question once and for all. He demanded the return of Danzig to the Reich and road and railway links through the Polish Corridor, in return for guaranteeing Poland's frontiers and a non-aggression pact.

Hitler's demands were rejected by the Poles. On 23rd May, Hitler told his High Command that Poland was to be attacked "at the first suitable opportunity" but with a note of caution that "it must not come to a simultaneous showdown in the west."

On 20th August, the world was stunned by the news that Russia and Germany had signed

a trade agreement. The same day Hitler demanded the annexation of Danzig. Three days later Russia and Germany signed a non-aggression pact undertaking not to attack each other and to remain neutral if either attacked a third power. There existed a second, secret part to the pact. Poland and the Baltic States were to be divided between them, Russia taking Estonia and Latvia, Germany getting Lithuania and Vilna. World reaction was immediate. America, France and Britain appealed for peace. Hitler interpreted this as an indication that the western allies were not prepared to fight for Poland.

On 23rd August, orders were issued to the Wermacht to invade Poland at dawn on the 26th. In the evening of the 25th, the orders were cancelled due to the fact that Mussolini had informed Hitler that Italy could not honour her commitments under the axis treaty and enter into a general European war without massive material and military aid from Germany. Simultaneously, Hitler received news that the Anglo-Polish treaty of 6th April 1939 was about to be ratified. On the 26th, Hitler took up the diplomatic initiative, but miscalculated in thinking that the outcome would be as Munich some twelve months previously. Daladier was still looking for a peaceful solution, though his Chiefs of Staff were ready to fight. In fact Daladier's floundering induced the Poles to delay mobilisation with the result that 25 per cent. of her army never reached the front. At 4 p.m. on the 31st, Hitler, making no progress with the British, issued orders that the invasion of Poland was to take place at dawn.

At 4.45 a.m. on Friday 1st September 1939, the old German battleship "Schleswig-Holstein" fired the first shots of World War II when she commenced a close-range bombardment of Polish coastal defences near Danzig. Simultaneously German troops crossed over the Polish frontier, and at 6.0 a.m. the Luftwaffe bombed Warsaw. At this late stage Britain and France, using Mussolini as an intermediary, said that they were willing to negotiate if German troops withdrew. Hitler, probably anticipating a short sharp war lasting only one or two weeks, rejected the proposal.

Throughout the towns and cities of Britain plans for the evacuation of young children, expectant mothers, the blind and the physically handicapped from areas likely to be bombed were put into operation.

That afternoon the War Office issued instructions to the Regular Army, Militia, Supplementary Reserve and the Territorial Army that general mobilisation had been proclaimed and that all troops should report to their units. Under the Defence Regulations the "blackout" came into force at sunset and would last 2,061 consecutive nights.

On Saturday 2nd September, Denmark, Finland, Iceland, Norway, Sweden, Latvia and Estonia declared their neutrality. Italy said that she would not take any initiative in military operations and Japan declared "By the conclusion of the non-aggression pact between Germany and the Soviet Union, Japan has been exempted from the obligation of supporting Germany if a second world war breaks out."

At 7.30 p.m. Chamberlain appeared before the House of Commons. The members expected to be told that an ultimatum had been delivered to Berlin. Instead they were told that there was still the possibility of a conference if Hitler would withdraw his troops. Chamberlain sat down to a silent house, no cheers, no applause. The acting Labour leader Arthur Greenwood rose to his feet. "Every minute's delay now means the loss of life, imperilling our national interests . . . imperilling the foundations of our national honour." The House broke up in confusion. The ministers Hore-Belisha, Anderson, de la Warr, Colville, Dorman-Smith, Stanley, Wallace and Elliott met with Sir John Simon in his room at the House. Later, Sir John went to see Chamberlain and delivered their message that war must be declared at once. The cabinet met at 11.0 a.m. The Anglo-French ultimatum was delivered at 9.0 a.m. Sunday 3rd September 1939 and expired two hours later without a German reply. Chamberlain spoke to the nation. We were at war.

PICTURE 8
Royal Artillery Territorials man a 3.7 inch AA heavy battery at Yardley, August 1939.

PICTURE 9A

Rehearsal for evacuation. St. George's School, Great Russell Street, Newtown, August 1939.

WARTIME BIRMINGHAM

Years before the outbreak of war the desirability for expansion of the warplane industry resulted in a government programme of extensions into this sphere for Birmingham motor firms. The new establishments were called shadow factories. Rover had one at Acocks Green, Austin at Cofton Hackett and Nuffield at Castle Bromwich. Other Birmingham factories adapted their engineering skills to the production of aircraft component parts.

It was primarily this aircraft industry that put Birmingham on the Luftwaffe's map, and the bombing was the major feature in the wartime experience of its citizens, which is why a substantial portion of this book is devoted to pictures of bomb damage.

Anticipating that this city, with its considerable engineering and munition industry, would lure the bombers, the government had made provision for the evacuation of large numbers of schoolchildren, and the day that Britain entered the war all schools were closed owing to the lack of air raid cover for the remaining children. It was months before all the surface brick shelters could be built in the school playgrounds.

Small groups of children were taught in local halls and in people's homes, and eventually, in the continuing absence of raids, some schools opened for voluntary attendance. In the general disruption there was considerable truancy, and education was an early casualty of the war.

The first air raid siren sounded in Birmingham on the night of 25th June 1940, but nothing happened. Birmingham was on the route for Coventry, Manchester and Liverpool, and out of the 367 times that alarms were to be sounded, only 77 would prove necessary.

The first bomb, from a lone raider, dropped in Erdington early in the morning of 9th August 1940, killing one man and injuring several other people. This bomb, like the majority that were to come, had missed its objective. The enemy's policy, so it was subsequently confirmed, was not to terrorise the people, but to damage factories and any vital public works. The hit-and-miss character of the bombing was due to technical inadequacy, but wrecked homes and human casualties a distance from factories naturally made people think it was deliberate. Even if terrorising had been the purpose, it was futile. The general spirit of defiance could sometimes be seen symbolised by a Union Jack stuck in a pile of rubble that was the remains of some family's home, and one man was seen securing an umbrella over his flag!

There were only minor attacks until the night of 25th/26th August, when the Market Hall burned out and 25 people died in the first raid on the city centre. Fort Dunlop was hit in daylight on 27th September and the Austin aero factory suffered a daylight raid on 13th November in wich 6 people died and 25 were injured, but the enemy did not develop this experiment and there was never more than minor daylight incursions.

The city centre was hit badly between 25th and 30th October. Incendiaries were used first. Fires could light up the scene ready for high explosives. Furthermore, there were not the number of people at hand in the city centre at night time to give immediate attention to every incendiary bomb that had penetrated a building. The Council House roof was damaged by fire and the Town Hall, the Art Gallery and the University (in Edmund Street) were also damaged. On the 25th 19 people in the Carlton Cinema in Taunton Road, Sparkhill were killed when a bomb exploded in front of the screen. It was on the 29th that the Cathedral suffered severe fire damage. Fortunately the prized Burne-Jones windows had already been moved to a place of safety.

The first massive raid, by 350 bombers, came on the 19th November. It lasted nearly all night, and on the 22nd another 200 bombers came. The attack was widespread. On the 19th B.S.A.'s factory at Small Heath was hit by high explosives and burned out. Nearly 50 employees were killed. Including lighter attacks on other nights, the casualties for the period from the 19th to the 28th were 796 dead and 2,345 injured. About 20,000 people were made homeless. A new weapon, the land mine, was being used. It was virtually a sea mine on a parachute and it was extremely powerful.

There followed a virtual lull until a very heavy raid on the night of 9th/10th April, 1941 — the last of its severity for the rest of the war. 250 raiders caused 1,121 casualties. High explosives damaged Birmingham Parish Church. There was little activity again until 27th July 1942 when between 60 and 70 bombers attacked in reprisal, on Hitler's orders, for the increasing intensity of our bombing of German cities.

There were no more very serious raids after this, the very last being on 23rd April 1943 when a mere two bombs fell on Bordesley Green, causing injuries, but no deaths. The last

siren sounded on the night of 15th May 1944.

The number of high explosives that had dropped on the city was 5,129 and in addition there were 48 parachute mines. Thousands of incendiaries had also showered down. The human toll for the blitz had been 2,241 dead, 3,010 seriously injured and 3,682 slightly injured. (The total fatalities in Britain for the whole war were 60,595 with 86,182 seriously injured.) Many casualties were among the services on duty during attacks, for they could not take cover.

For all the devastation, the air war on Birmingham did not achieve its purpose. Vital industries suffered some disruption, but the overall effect on the city's industrial war effort was negligible. The Luftwaffe was not equipped for the sustained, long-range heavy bombing such as Bomber Command was. In Hamburg 20,000 people were killed in one raid alone.

Birmingham made very important contributions to the war effort in the field of scientific achievement. Under Sir Mark Oliphant at the University, Professor Jones and a research team perfected the resonant cavity magnetron valve, which greatly increased the power of radar. This was invaluable in detecting both bomber and submarine.

Uranium was first worked in this country at the I.C.I. (now I.M.I.) laboratory at Witton and Sir Mark Oliphant was also a member of the Birmingham research team that solved fundamental problems of making the atomic bomb, taking their knowledge to America. The jet engine benefited greatly from the development of a nickel-chromium alloy for the turbine blades, enabling them to withstand the highest temperature involved in their functioning. This was the achievement of the Mond Nickel Research Department, now the Inco Euro Research establishment in Wiggin Street, Ladywood.

One of the dreariest aspects of everyday life during the war was the "blackout," which came into force on 1st September 1939. Everybody had to keep their windows covered inside during darkness so that no chink of artificial light would show through. Vehicles had shields over the top of their headlamps. With no street lighting, people used small torches in the streets. Petrol was rationed. Public transport was severely curtailed and the long waiting in darkness for a bus was depressing. Searchlight beams played across the night sky.

There was drabness and difficulty in daytime too. In May 1940 when a paratroop invasion was feared, all place-name signs on premises were covered over, and signposts were removed. Barrage balloons continually marred an aesthetic appreciation of the sky. The sounding of church bells was reserved as a warning that paratroops were dropping.

All kinds of precautions were thought of. Factories were painted with a design that camouflaged them. Edgbaston reservoir was drained low, as its reflection in moonlight made it a landmark, and furthermore it constituted a flooding threat if its dam were broken.

In order to keep food imports to a minimum restrictions were imposed. The manager of the Express Cafe in Moor Street was fined £2 for contravening regulations by supplying bacon and egg — to a food inspector, and a man in Smethwick was fined £5 6s 0d for wasting food because he threw a hip-bone steak at a neighbour's door.

A typical example of the wry humour of the time was the shop window slogan that read, "Keep smiling. The Nazis won't come here. We serve only the best people."

A pointer to the extremes to which the public were exhorted to economise is the following that appeared in the "Sunday Mercury" in November 1942:

"SPARE THE POKER THIS WINTER. Anything that makes a fire burn faster than it needs — whether in grate or boiler — is an act of sabotage against the nation's stout effort to save fuel."

PICTURE 10

Canon Norman Power, Vicar of Ladywood: "I was in the back of our house in Summerfield Crescent, Edgbaston, when I heard the whine of the bomb. I grabbed my camera, held it up above my head, opened the shutter and took this picture of the bomb landing in the middle of the reservoir."

EVACUATION

PICTURE 11
A loudspeaker van, in the Handsworth area, announcing the evacuation of schoolchildren in 1939.

The areas in Birmingham from which schoolchildren were to be evacuated were the central ones and those containing munition works. On 20th July 1939, 9 schools took part in an evacuation rehearsal at Hockley G.W.R. Station, and on 28th August there was a fuller rehearsal. On 31st August special messengers advised the schools that the evacuation would take place next day, a Friday.

Most parties were within marching distance of a railway station, but over 240 buses had been reserved to take 15,000 from their assembly points. Approximately 73,000 children were involved in this voluntary scheme, but only a third of this number presented themselves on the day, this proportion being reflected throughout the country.

Nearly every train started from Snow Hill, New Street or Moor Street, picking up parties at stations on the way. The children were equipped with lunch packs, gas masks and name tags on their blazers, and were accompanied by over 4,000 teachers and helpers.

The authorities kept the destinations secret even from the parents. Some tearful mothers who had gone to see their children off took them back home again.

The dispersal was in all directions, the destinations near and far. Boulton Road Junior School, Handsworth, for instance, went no further

than Hagley, while the children of St. Benedict's Road School, Small Heath went to Ross-on-Wye, to be accommodated there and in the surrounding villages. No child, however, was to be more than 3½ hours' journey away.

The following day mothers with very small children, numbering 12,377 in all were evacuated along with 406 expectant mothers and 20 handicapped adults.

As it happened, evacuation day coincided with Germany's attack on Poland, and two days later, when Britain declared war, parents of children remaining changed their minds, and there was such a clamour for evacuation that the Education Department stayed open all week-end for several weeks.

As the weeks passed with no bombing, evacuees began to drift back, and this continued throughout the "phoney" war, although new evacuees were taking their places. Many schools had officially returned when the first bomb fell on the city in August 1940, and in the renewed anxiety there was re-evacuation for many.

After the holocaust of the night of 22nd/23rd November, which left the east side of the city waterless, a further mass exodus was arranged. On 26th November 8,343 children departed with 763 teachers and by 10th December another 13,705 children left. Strong representations to the Ministry of Health resulted in the entire city being declared "evacuable" and in March, 1941, there were nearly 20,000 official evacuees besides the estimated 20,000 who had gone privately, many to relatives. At the end of 1944 the full-scale permanent return began.

In its turn Birmingham played host to thousands of mothers and children from London and the Southern Counties as from July 1944, after flying-bomb attacks had begun.

Ruby Massa:
"I was evacuated twice from Saltley Grammar School. On the second occasion, in November 1940, 60 of us children were sent to Hinckley along with 5 of our teachers. We were herded onto Hinckley School stage and the local children were asked to pick one evacuee each to take home. I had a lovely new life with a Methodist lay preacher and his family, but there was quite a lot of resentment from some of the young Hinckleyites towards us Brummies."

PICTURE 12
The exodus to the safe areas is under way.

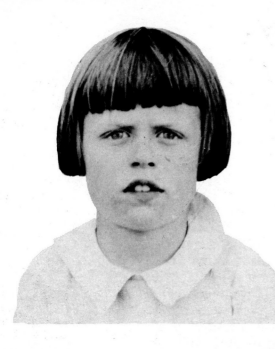

PICTURE 13

Pat Cotton: *"My brother and I lived in Felixstowe, but were evacuated to Birmingham in 1940, and assembled with other children at Silver Street school. He was six and I was nine but he had to take care of me because I was deaf and dumb. We cried and cried, when they tried to part us, because he was the only one who could understand me, and so we were the last ones to be chosen. Eventually a kind lady, Mrs. Bromwich, from Packhorse Lane, Wythall, took me and her neighbour took my brother and so we were able to live next door to each other."* Pat is now Mrs. Hatfield, happily married, living in Warstock and has learned to communicate by lip reading.

PICTURE 14

1939. Wardens, wearing tin hats, escort young evacuees at Moor Street Station.

HOME FRONT

Despite the general unease facing Europe since the Czech crisis, little was done by the British Government to build up reserves of food, fuel and essential raw materials. As the Second World War loomed ever closer both the Cabinet and the Admiralty considered that the main threat to our merchant ships would come from German surface raiders. The submarine threat, whilst not being overlooked, was pushed into the background, too much faith being placed on asdic, the Navy's anti-submarine detection device. Whilst asdic was a remarkable piece of equipment it was not as efficient as many people had been led to believe.

In September 1939, the German U-boat Arm comprised 56 submarines of which only 22 were ocean-going boats capable of operating in the Atlantic. When hostilities commenced every available U-boat was already deployed on its respective war station. In the first month of the war 40 merchant and fishing vessels were sunk by U-boats, 9 vessels were sunk by mine, and only one, the ''Clement,'' was sunk by a surface raider. In all 189,000 tons of shipping was sent to the bottom. By the end of the year the U-boats had claimed 103 victims, 83 vessels had been sunk by mine, 15 by surface raiders and 10 by the Luftwaffe — a grand total of 746,000 tons.

On 27th September, Sir John Simon introduced the Emergency War Budget and the first commodity to be rationed was petrol. An increase in whisky duty was expected to bring in £3,500,000 in a full year. The basic duty on tobacco was increased from 11s 6d to 13s 6d per pound, adding 1½d per ounce to the price in the shops. Sugar duty was increased by 1d per pound and that led directly to price increases on tinned fruit, jam, marmalade, syrup and sweetened milk.

The rationing of basic foodstuffs was introduced in January 1940. Weekly allowances per person included 2oz butter, 4oz sugar, 2oz tea (none for the under fives), 2oz sweets, 2oz fats. Extra cheese was allowed for persons who had no canteen facilities at their place of work. In 1941 the ''points'' system was introduced for clothing and tinned meats. Cigarettes and tobacco were not officially rationed, but tobacconists would often sell only to regulars. Monday 21st April 1941 witnessed queues outside Birmingham tobacconists due to the acute shortage. Notices outside many shops simply read ''No cigarettes, no tobacco, no sweets.'' A week later a supply of oranges was on sale, though only about 1 in 5 of the population eventually got any, the majority being reserved for young children.

At the beginning of 1945, the weekly basic ration was 4oz bacon, 2oz tea, 8oz sugar, meat to the value of 1s 2d (about 1lb.), 8oz fats, 3oz cheese, 2 pints of milk (later increased to 2½ pints).

The astonishing fact is that the health of the nation as a whole improved during the war. Rations were in small proportions, but sufficient. School meals were provided for children, expectant mothers and young children were allowed extra milk, oranges (when available), orange juice, eggs, cod liver oil and vitamin tablets. Factory workers benefited from works canteens and local authorities set up British Restaurants to provide cheap meals to the general public. Also, people were encouraged to grow their own vegetables on allotments.

In 1945 the clothing ration was 48 coupons. A man's suit cost 24 coupons, work shirts 5 coupons, men's trousers 5 coupons, ladies' dresses 11 coupons, children's gaberdine raincoats 12 coupons.

Besides rations and allotment produce the black market was a source of commodities — at a price. Whisky cost £5 a bottle, petrol 4 shillings a gallon, clothing coupons 2-5 shillings each and sugar was one shilling per pound.

16

PICTURE 16 December 1940. Sorting some of the
millions of Birmingham area ration books ready for posting.

PICTURE 17 Queueing for ration books at the
Civic Centre, 18th May 1943.

17

RATIONING

of Clothing, Cloth & Footwear *from* June 1

When the shops re-open you will be able to buy cloth, clothes, footwear and knitting wool *only if you bring your Food Ration Book with you*. The shopkeeper will detach the required number of coupons from the unused margarine page. Each margarine coupon counts as one coupon towards the purchase of clothing or footwear. You will have a total of 66 coupons to last you for a year; so go sparingly.

Remember you can buy *where* you like and *when* you like without registering.

NUMBER OF COUPONS NEEDED

MEN and BOYS

	Adult	Child
Unlined mackintosh or cape ...	9	7
Other mackintoshes, or raincoat, or overcoat	16	11
Coat, or jacket, or blazer or like garment	13	8
Waistcoat, or pull-over, or cardigan, or jersey	5	3
Trousers (other than fustian or corduroy)	8	6
Fustian or corduroy trousers ...	5	5
Shorts	5	3
Overalls, or dungarees or like garment	6	4
Dressing-gown or bathing-gown ...	8	6
Night-shirt or pair of pyjamas ...	8	6
Shirt, or combinations—woollen ...	8	6
Shirt, or combinations—other material	5	4
Pants, or vest, or bathing costume, or child's blouse	4	2
Pair of socks or stockings ...	3	1
Collar, or tie, or pair of cuffs ...	1	1
Two handkerchiefs ...	1	1
Scarf, or pair of gloves or mittens	2	2
Pair of slippers or goloshes ...	4	2
Pair of boots or shoes ...	7	3
Pair of leggings, gaiters or spats	3	2

WOMEN and GIRLS

	Adult	Child
Lined mackintoshes, or coats (over 28 in. length)	14	11
Jacket, or short coat (under 28 in. in length)	11	8
Dress, or gown, or frock—woollen ...	11	8
Dress, or gown, or frock—other material	7	5
Gym. tunic, or girl's skirt with bodice	8	6
Blouse, or sports shirt, or cardigan, or jumper	5	3
Skirt, or divided skirt ...	7	5
Overalls, or dungarees or like garment	6	4
Apron, or pinafore ...	3	2
Pyjamas ...	8	6
Nightdress ...	6	5
Petticoat, or slip, or combinations, or cami-knickers	4	3
Other undergarments, including corsets	3	2
Pair of stockings ...	2	1
Pair of socks (ankle length) ...	1	1
Collar, or tie, or pair of cuffs ...	1	1
Two handkerchiefs ...	1	1
Scarf, or pair of gloves or mittens, or muff	2	2
Pair of slippers, boots or shoes	5	3

CLOTH. Coupons needed per yard depend on the width. For example, a yard of woollen cloth 36 inches wide requires 3 coupons.

The same amount of cotton or other cloth needs 2 coupons.

KNITTING WOOL. 1 coupon for two ounces.

Extra coupons for bombed persons

Those who receive advances of money from the Assistance Board or the Department of Customs and Excise to enable them to replace clothing or footwear will receive at the same time extra coupons.

Goods by Post

If you are ordering goods by post you must cut out the proper number of coupons yourself, sign your name on the back and send them with the order. Otherwise coupons must be detached only by the shopkeeper.

THESE GOODS MAY BE BOUGHT *WITHOUT* COUPONS

¶ Children's clothing, of sizes generally suitable for infants less than 4 years old. ¶ Boiler suits and workmen's bib and brace overalls. ¶ Hats and caps. ¶ Sewing thread. ¶ Mending wool and mending silk. ¶ Boot and shoe laces. ¶ Tapes, braids, ribbons and other fabrics of 3 inches or less in width. ¶ Elastic. ¶ Lace and lace net. ¶ Sanitary towels. ¶ Braces, suspenders and garters. ¶ Hard haberdashery. ¶ Clogs. ¶ Black-out cloth dyed black. ¶ All second-hand articles.

ISSUED BY THE BOARD OF TRADE

FOOD FACTS

POINTS GUIDE April 4th —May 1st

BISCUITS
Plain	1 point per lb.
Sweet	4 points ,,
Chocolate	8 ,, ,,

Broken Biscuits are half the above values.

CEREAL BREAKFAST FOODS
2, 3 or 4 points per package according to size
Rolled Oats (loose or in packets) . 1 point per 8 oz.

CONDENSED MILK
Full Cream sweetened . 4 or 8 points according to size
Full Cream unsweetened; Skimmed,
1 or 2 points according to size

FISH (*canned*)
Crawfish	24 points per lb.

Herring, Mackerel, Pilchard—
1's oval . . .	6 ,, ,, tin
1's tall . . .	4 ,, ,, ,,
½'s oval & round . .	3 ,, ,, ,,
5 oz. . . .	2 ,, ,, ,,

Salmon	Grades 1 and 2	Grade 3
1's tall & flat	32	4 points per tin
½'s flat	20	4 ,, ,, ,,
¼'s flat	10	2 ,, ,, ,,

Sardines, American or Canadian . 2 ,, ,, ,,
Portuguese . . 3-7 points for usual sizes
10-36 points for large sizes

For the point values of other canned or bottled fish, see the Ministry of Food's *Retail Price List*.

FRUIT (*imported and home-produced, canned*)
Large tins . . .	12 points per tin
Medium tins . . .	9 ,, ,, ,,
Small tins . . .	6 ,, ,, ,,

FRUIT (*dried*)
Prunes . . .	4 points per lb.
Figs	6 ,, ,, ,,
Dates	12 ,, ,, ,,
Sultanas, Currants and any other dried fruit . .	16 ,, ,, ,,

MEAT (*canned*)
Minced Meat Loaf . .	18 points per 12 oz.
Canned Pork Sausage Meat .	9 ,, ,, 1½ lb.
Stewed Steak . .	24 ,, ,, 1 lb.
Canned Rabbit 20 points per 1 lb.	32 points per 2 lb.
Ready or prepared meals .	8 ,, ,, lb.
Tongues, Briskets, Pressed Beef	24 ,, ,, 12 oz.
Luncheon Meat, Pork or Ham Loaf	18 ,, ,, 12 oz.

Other sizes 24 points upwards
Luncheon Meat sold sliced . . 16 points per lb.
Meat Roll or Galantine 1, 4 or 5 points according to size
When sold sliced . . . 2 points per lb.

PEAS, BEANS, LENTILS (*dried*)
Haricot Beans . .	1 point per lb.
Lentils, Split Peas, Peas .	2 points per lb.

RICE, SAGO, TAPIOCA . . 4 points per lb.

SYRUP, TREACLE . . . 8 ,, ,, ,,

VEGETABLES (*canned*)
Beans, baked, in Tomato Sauce 2-8 points according to size
Peas A2½, A2 and A1 tall tins . 4 points per tin
A1 and E1 tins . . . 3 ,, ,, ,,
Tomatoes (where available) 3-9 points according to size

The total number of points per person remains at 20. A = 1 B = 2 C = 2

CUT THIS OUT AND KEEP IT!

THE MINISTRY OF FOOD, LONDON, W.1. FOOD FACTS No. 144

PICTURE 20

A bombed house in Aston miraculously becomes a W.V.S. cafe at the War Office Training School in 1942.

PICTURE 21

A blitz canteen and tea and buns supplied by the W.V.S. who, as always, were there to give comfort and help where it was most needed.

PICTURE 22

13th October 1941. A mobile canteen presented by Michigan, one of the 11 other Birminghams in America, to serve people "bombed out" and rescue squads. Mrs. Margo Millington, who provided this photograph, can be seen peering out of the open hatch.

23

PICTURE 23

The coalman cometh to the Cobden Hotel, Cherry Street, City Centre in January 1940.

24

PICTURE 24

The bad weather proved to be an added hazard. The corner of Mansfield Road and Tiffield Road, Acocks Green, January 1940.

25

PICTURE 25
Tram 3 on Route 6 (Perry Barr) after having its windows blown out by a bomb blast at Miller Street Depot, April 1941. This was one of the results of a direct hit on the Perry Barr section of the depot.

PICTURE 26
Tram 664 on Route 2 (Erdington and Steelhouse Lane). Note houses in background with the top half of their windows boarded up following bomb blast damage. 13th June 1941.

26

PICTURE 27
Midland Red gas-producing trailer attachment, to overcome the petrol shortage, 25th August 1942.

PICTURE 28
To prevent the devastation that occurred at many of the bus depots, some vehicles were parked overnight a distance away. To avoid freezing up, these buses are coupled up to immersion heaters in Fox Hollies Road, Acocks Green. Note the radiator muffs and leads (arrowed), 6th February 1942.

PICTURE 29
Boy Scouts cart soldiers' luggage between Snow Hill and New Street stations, March 1943.

PICTURE 30
Boys' Brigade Messenger Service at the ready.

PICTURE 31
As always, the Salvation Army were in the thick of things, helping out wherever there was a need.

Lend a hand

on the land

at a Volunteer Agricultural Camp

The world is faced with a food shortage. Our farmers and farmworkers are doing their best to make sure we don't go without. But volunteer help is needed — more than ever this year — if we are not to go short. It's YOUR help that's needed on the farms. So spend your holiday at a farm camp.

It's hard work but it's healthy; there'll be good fun in the evenings. Pay 1/- an hour minimum; accommodation 28/- a week. (● *Volunteers under 18 not accepted*).

More than 40 camps have been arranged in the counties of Hereford, Leicester, Montgomery, Northampton, Nottingham, Oxford, Rutland, Stafford, Warwick and Worcester. At least 25,000 volunteers are wanted between 1st April and 31st October. Help at the start and end of season specially needed. So don't delay . . .

✦ Post coupon now to :-

The Regional Organiser,
    Volunteer Agricultural Camps (Midlands),
        11, Edmund Street,
            BIRMINGHAM.   Tel. Midland 0461

PLEASE SEND PARTICULARS OF YOUR CAMPS TO :

NAME..

ADDRESS..

.... C.3

INDUSTRY AT WAR

The effect on industry at the outset of the war was limited. The reason, of course, was the absence of any major confrontation with the Germans except at sea. During this period, known as the "phoney" war, the Government actively encouraged firms to continue exporting their products. As the war became more intense, especially after the fall of France, Britain began moving towards a total war economy and thousands of firms, large and small alike, were given Government contracts.

Cadbury's, at Bournville, for example, continued to produce its world-famous chocolate-based products but, following Government instruction, undertook other work as well, such as the manufacture of aircraft parts, including hydraulic pressure bodies, radiator flap jacks, dive brake assemblies and vertical milling machines. Jewellers and silversmiths transferred their skill to the making of component parts for radar equipment, rifles and aeroplanes. Blind people were employed at S.U. Carburettors, using their sense of touch for certain inspection jobs.

As with the First World War heavy industry found itself having to employ women in both semi-skilled and highly skilled jobs.

PICTURE 33
Women workers at a BSA dispersal unit with a belt of ammunition for a Browning gun. The Browning had a theoretical rate of fire of 1,200 rounds per minute.

PICTURE 34
Colmore Row, 1940.

PICTURE 35
Four of the lady welders who produced ammunition boxes at Parkinson Cowan, 1942. The factory also produced fuses for 3.7 and 4.7 shells, Mills hand grenades, cast iron weights for mines, incendiary bomb cases, jerry cans and air/sea rescue radio survival kits, etc.

27

POST ✠ OFFICE
TELEGRAM

FROM AIRPROD AP 784 25/4

I CALL UPON THE AIRCRAFT INDUSTRY TO MAKE A SUPREME EFFORT
CASUALTIES LAST WEEK ONCE MORE EXCEEDED PRODUCTION

AT A MOMENT WHEN THE PUBLIC HAVE LEARNED WITH SO MUCH
SATISFACTION OF THE RESERVES WHICH YOU HAVE BUILT UP FOR THE
ROYAL AIR FORCE WE ARE COMPELLED TO MAKE INROADS UPON THAT
RESERVE STRENGTH

IT IS FOR THE INDUSTRY THE MANAGEMENT AND STAFFS THE MEN AND
WOMEN WHO WORK IN THE FACTORIES TO SUSTAIN AND HUSBAND THIS
VITAL SOURCE OF REINFORCEMENT FOR OUR BATTLE LINE

WHAT CAN YOU DO TO HELP IN URGENT TASK

BEAVERBROOK

PICTURE 37
Wing assemblies for Beaufighters

PICTURE 38
Wing assemblies for Miles Master aircraft.

PICTURE 39

Fairey Battle aircraft under construction at Austin.

29

PICTURE 40
Spitfire production at Castle Bromwich
Aeroplane Factory.

PICTURE 41
Fuselage sections of Stirling bombers under
construction.

CANTEEN SERVICE

The new CANTEEN will be OPEN MONDAY NEXT, SEPT. 29th. Those wishing to have Dinners on that day should purchase their tickets from the Canteen on Saturday Sept. 27th

The following prices will be Charged in the Canteen

Meat 2 Vegetables, Bread		10d & 11d
Fish	„ „	10d
Boiled Pudding & Cutard		3d
Milk „ „		3d
Stewed Fruit „		3d
Cakes		1½d & 2d
Tea	per ½ pint	1d
Coffee or Cocoa	„	1½d

Employees should note that they are expected to provide their own Knife, Fork & Spoon

"B'Mail" 10/10/40 LOAD THE GUNS

Next week is Birmingham's War Weapons Week. £8,000,000 in war savings is the total aimed at.

PICTURE 44 Putting the finishing touches to military ambulances.

45

PICTURE 45
The end of the Austin
assembly line for Churchill
tank bogies.

PICTURE 46A
Shells transferred from the
turning machine onto a
truck.

46A

PICTURE 46B AND 46C

Crusader tanks under construction, August 1941. They were made at Nuffield Mech. & Aero Ltd., Washwood Heath, Morris Commercial Cars, Adderley Park, and M. B. Wild & Co. Ltd., Nechells.

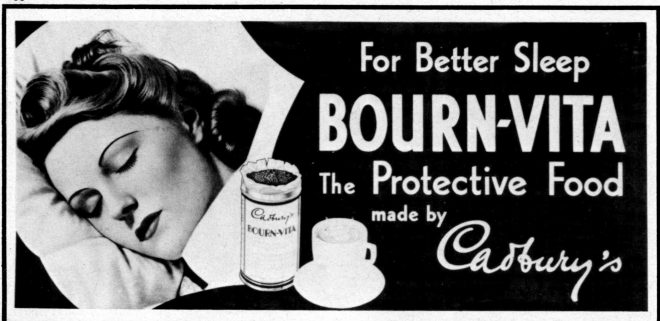

PICTURE 48

Camouflage in progress at U block, Cadbury's, 1940. Mrs. Joyce Cadbury: "The police came to our house in Hole Lane, Northfield, and warned us that because two unexploded landmines were in trees nearby, we should leave all our windows open. After sitting in our lounge, in freezing weather, for some time, we decided that the cold was worse than the Germans, so we closed the windows. After a short interval one of the bombs went off, opening all our windows for us — including some that had not been open in 30 years! Remarkably not a single pane of glass was broken."

PICTURE 49 Salvaged tins of condensed milk, from the Coventry blitz, being checked at Cadbury's, for the Ministry of Food.

PICTURE 52
Dismantling the Cathedral railings for salvage. A great deal of this metal was found to be completely unusable.

MAKE IT A REAL BLACK-OUT

From 7.47 p.m. to 6.14 a.m. to-night complete observance of the lighting restrictions is vital to public safety.

At every house, business or manufacturing premises, and public utility undertaking, some responsible person should make an inspection of the building immediately after 7.47 p.m. to see that the Blackout is completely effective.

After this, outside doors should not be left open, unless a light-trap is provided, and lights should not be switched on in rooms where Blackout provision has not been made.

Publicans and shopkeepers please take special note.

Motorists should, as far as possible, avoid travelling, and if they are obliged to be on the roads, should faithfully observe the lighting restrictions.

NEGLECT OF THESE PRECAUTIONS BY ANY PERSONS MAY INVOLVE SERIOUS LOSS OF LIFE.

Joe Russell: "Owing to the blackout and devastation it was very difficult for bus conductors and passengers to tell when a destination had been reached, so the transport people asked for volunteers to act as auxiliary conductors. I worked in Dale End at Young, Waterhouse and Co., mainly producing submarine parts, and I volunteered. We were issued with armbands and travelled free on the buses, calling out the names of the streets and landmarks as we reached the various destinations."

CIVIL DEFENCE

At the height of the bombing approximately 1½ million people in Britain were involved in Air Raid Precaution work. About 80% were part-time volunteers and nearly 25% were women.

The A.R.P. Warden's job was essentially in two separate parts. He had to judge the extent and type of damage in his area so that the Control Centre could send the appropriate rescue services. His local knowledge was vital if time was to be saved hunting for survivors trapped beneath debris. Secondly, he was responsible for getting the bombed-out to some sort of shelter or a Rest Centre.

Ninety per cent. of wardens were part-timers and one in six was a woman. There were normally six wardens to a post, and one post to every 500 people.

First Aid Posts were usually manned by a doctor, a trained nurse and nursing auxiliaries. There was normally one F.A.P. to every 15,000 people. There were also mobile units used to reinforce a hard pressed fixed post or even a hospital.

Under the orders of a Control Centre a First Aid Party consisted of four men and a driver and all were experienced First Aid workers, having been trained by either the Red Cross, St. John or St. Andrew's Society. The party's first task was to help the Rescue Men release trapped casualties and then to administer what aid they could before deciding whether or not a casualty needed further treatment either at a post or at a hospital.

The task of Rescue Men was the really back-breaking work, often amid fire and the ever present danger of explosion from fractured gas pipes, searching the debris for both victims and survivors.

The A.R.P. organisation embraced many others, ranging from the Police and the Fire Service to the Women's Voluntary Service, who in the early stages looked after the bombed-out as well as manning mobile canteens and Rest Centres. In Birmingham members of the Boys' Brigade acted as A.R.P. messengers and were often the main channel of communication between the services. The city's Civil Defence Headquarters was at the Council House, the Clock Tower being used as an observation post.

GAS ATTACK

55

54

PICTURE 54

In February, 1940, this fearsome creature was quite a common sight — a friendly A.R.P. warden with a rattle which acted as a primitive early-warning system. It was a widely held opinion that the Germans would use gas against civilians. This did not materialise.

PICTURE 56

Telephonists ready for a possible gas attack. The mask had a built-in microphone which plugged into the side of their mouthpiece.

PICTURE 57

Jack Warner, touring with his show "Garrison Theatre," takes time out at Birmingham Hippodrome to christen a new A.F.S. trailer pump "Little Gel." The comedian/actor, who later became known to millions as Dixon of Dock Green, always referred to Joan Winters, seen here, as his "little gel." September 1940.

PICTURE 58

Auxiliary firemen taking the field at the County Ground at Edgbaston in December 1939. Normally the home of Warwickshire County Cricket Club, it was used as an A.F.S. station at the time. Leslie Deakins, secretary, Warks. C.C.C., 1944-76: "Actually the A.F.S. were responsible for first installing electricity for light purposes there. I returned home from leave to find that the only direct hit was a high explosive bomb that had landed on the practice shed, which also served as the players' luncheon room."

59

60

61

PICTURE 59

Men of A.F.S. station 41.C1.

PICTURE 60

The staff at Edgbaston High School for Girls formed their own A.F.S. unit and are shown here practising with the assistance of the school caretaker, June 1940.

PICTURE 61

Auxiliary water tank in Victoria Square, September 3, 1939. Tanks were placed at strategic points around the city to provide the fire service with a supply of water in the event of the mains being put out of action.

63

Councillor Tiptaft complains that some people are not only leaving their own shelters to go to public shelters but are taking beds bedding, perambulators and virtually everything except the old kitchen stove with them.

64

PICTURE 65

An enormous surface shelter in the Old Square. Lewis's store is on the right. John Clarke, BBC Midlands TV Producer: "As a boy of eight my mother took me to nearby Crane's to buy me a ukelele. A notice on the window read 'Musical instruments will only be sold to members of H.M. Forces'. Knowing my passion for music, she asked for an instrument for her eldest son in the Royal Navy. When the assistant requested more information, she turned to me and said out loud, "What sort of 'uke' do you want then?"

PICTURE 66
Workers at the Wolseley Sheep Shearing Machine Company, Witton,
self-consciously posing for this 1939 publicity photo in one of their nine
reinforced concrete air-raid shelters. The hand-operated fresh air system
was simply comprised of a fan sucking down air through a tube from above.

PICTURE 67
A back court shelter
in Winson Street,
Winson Green.

68

PICTURE 68 The first Birmingham policeman to be awarded the George Medal for gallantry during the blitz was P.C. Ronald Jackson. Fourth from the right, he stands in line to meet the P.M., Winston Churchill, in September 1941.

PICTURE 69
A mock accident in the yard at Digbeth Police School as further training for Police War Reserves in 1943. Spot the blackout mask on the car headlamp?

69

WITNESS FOR
PROSECUTION

PROSECUTING
SOLICITOR

WITNESS
BOX

WITNESS
BOX

PRISONER.

MAGISTRATE

MAGISTRATE'S
CLERK

DOCK

DEFENDING
SOLICITOR

WITNESS FOR
DEFENCE

PICTURE 70
Training of Police War
Reserves. A mock court held
in the top floor classroom at
Digbeth Police School in
1943.

44

PICTURE 71

A 1943 police display in Lewis's, Corporation Street, advertises the new two-way radios for patrol cars. The public were encouraged to dial CEN 5000 for police assistance. (The "999" system did not operate in Birmingham until 1946.)

PICTURE 72

Rain-drenched factory roof spotters on duty in relays for 24 hours a day. The man in the doorway is responsible for phoning through reports of any enemy aircraft spotted. November 1942.

PICTURE 73

Home Secretary Sir John Anderson (centre) inspects decontamination men at the Central Car Park, January 1940. The Chief A.R.P. Officer, Mr. Hamilton, with one eye on the camera, accompanies him.

73

PICTURE 74

Ready for any emergency. "E" Division A.R.P. Wardens, c1943.

PICTURE 75

Time for relaxation. "E" Division A.R.P. Wardens with families and friends at St. Paul's Ballroom, Balsall Heath in 1942.

76

77

78

79

PICTURE 77
The despatch riders of the Piers Road A.R.P. Depot, Handsworth. They were kept busy carrying messages when the telephone wires were down and acting as guides for ambulances in the bombed areas, October 1940.

PICTURE 78
An A.R.P. telephone operator in the underground control room at Fort Dunlop, September 1939.

PICTURE 79
The underground A.R.P. telephone exchange at Stechford, May 1940.

PICTURE 80

The Duke and Duchess of Gloucester visit the Civil Defence Depot Central Car Park, January 14, 1943.

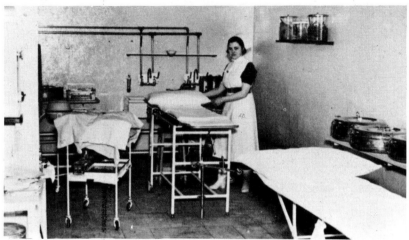

PICTURE 81

An operating theatre in Lewis's basement. There was also one in Ansell's basement.

PICTURE 82

Everything ready at the Queen's Hospital, October 20, 1939. In 1941 it became the Birmingham Accident Hospital.

PICTURE 83 Bomb snuffers at the ready, July 3, 1940.
This must surely be one of the most mind-boggling pictures of the era!

THE MILITARY

Home Guard

On 14th May 1940, Anthony Eden, then Secretary of State for War, broadcast an appeal for men between 17 and 65 to form a new force whose primary function would be to guard factories, railways, canals and other vital points, and to oppose enemy paratroops.

In Birmingham, as elsewhere, the response was overwhelming. Long queues formed outside the enrolment centres, some of which ran out of application forms. Applicants offered the use of their bicycles, motor-cycles and cars.

Until there were enough rifles, drill was done with broomsticks and imitation wooden rifles. Even uniforms were not available at the start. The force was called the Local Defence Volunteers, but after Mr. Churchill had referred to them as the Home Guard, this became their official name in July.

In due course there was training with machine guns, mortars and hand grenades. Birmingham factories important to the war effort formed companies from their own personnel to guard their premises, as did the Council House and the Gas, Water, Electricity and Salvage Departments, for sabotage attempts were always a possibility.

On one occasion men saved the Council House by extinguishing incendiaries, and three of the Salvage Department Company were killed in a raid while on duty at the Montague Street works.

At its peak Birmingham's Home Guard numbered 53,000. The organisation stood down on 1st November 1944.

PICTURE 84 Wolseley Motors unit in 1940. Note the grim purposefulness of the men — and the wooden rifles.

PICTURE 85
52nd Warks (B'ham) bn., leaving Chelsea Barracks, London, after a training visit which lasted from 30th April to 2nd May 1943. They are led by pipers from the Scots Guards.

85

PICTURE 86
Commissioned Officers, 52nd Warks (B'ham) bn., Castle Bromwich Aeroplane Factory, September 1944. Maurice Price 2nd Lt. Home Guard (6th right, back row): "Leaving my job at Castle Bromwich Aeroplane Factory one night in thick fog and a total blackout, I acted as guide and walked in front of the bus all the way to the Fox and Goose at Ward End. There the fog cleared, so I boarded the bus, only to be charged the full fare from Castle Bromwich."

86

PICTURE 87 Somewhere in the heart of Harborne Dad's Army did their bit for King and Country. "C" and "D" Company Signallers of the 21st Birmingham Battallion.

87

PICTURE 88 *Rocket Projection Drill, July 1942. This picture was originally banned from publication by the censor.*

PICTURE 89
A street fighting school in Aston.

PICTURE 90 *Visit of General Montgomery to Birmingham, 9th March 1944.*

PICTURE 91 *Stand-down parade in December 1944.*

PICTURE 92
One of the 3.7inch anti-aircraft guns defending Birmingham, May 1940.

93

94

95

PICTURE 96
March past of the Royal
Warks. Regt. at the Hall of
Memory, Broad Street,
October 1940.

YOUR CITY MUS' RAISE

57

MINESWEEPER ASTON VILLA

The Minesweeper Aston Villa, which has been "adopted" by the Aston and Lozells women's working parties. The first consignment of gifts to the crew have already been sent.

PICTURE 97

H.M.S. Birmingham. Southampton Class cruiser of 9,100 tons (12,000 tons full load) built at Devonport. Completed in 1937, she served throughout the war. Bruce Normansell (Able-seaman, H.M.S. Birmingham May-September 1941): "I felt a great deal of concern leaving Birmingham after the heavy raids, but there were a lot of Brummies aboard, and we all knew that there was an important job to be done elsewhere." At the time his father F. M. Normansell, was Chairman of Aston Villa and councillor for Lozells.

PICTURE 98

H.M.S. Aston Villa. Completed 1937 and requisitioned by the Royal Navy in 1939. She was attacked by enemy aircraft on 3rd May 1940, whilst operating off Norway, and was scuttled several hours later.

PICTURE 99

Royal National lifeboat "The Guide of Dunkirk," paid for by the Girl Guide movement, took part in the evacuation of Dunkirk.

100

PICTURE 101 ATS driver directing a breakdown lorry which has come to her assistance after a skid into a roadside ditch during the bad weather of February 1941.

PICTURE 102
A line-up of Army vehicles with ATS drivers, February 1941.

PICTURE 103 *Jewish members of the forces outside Singers Hill Synagogue after one of the monthly services, organised by the Jewish Hospitality Community, 1943.*

PICTURE 104
Salute the Soldier. A United States military band in New Street 22nd June 1944.

PICTURE 105 *Salute the Soldier. U.S. troops parade along New Street, 22nd June 1944. The photograph is taken from the first floor window of the old Birmingham Post and Mail building in New Street (almost opposite the Midland Hotel).*

REFUGEES
from Nazi Oppression
present

A Performance given by
Austrian, Czech, German
and Spanish refugees . .

ASTON HIPPODROME
SUNDAY, 7th DECEMBER, at 2-45 p.m. 1941

Two Shillings and Sixpence
(Including Tax)

PROGRAMME NOTES

Song of the Marsh Soldiers

Created and secretly sung by the prisoners of a notorious Nazi Concentration Camp

The song has since become a kind of anti-Fascist anthem throughout the world. It describes the monotony of the marshes and the rigour of the camps; it concludes with a firm belief in final liberation.

Song of the Workers of Vienna

Sung by millions of Austrian workers at their meetings

The Chorus says:

"We are the faithful fighters for the future; we the workers of Vienna."

March of the Red Cavalry

An Original Russian Song

It praises the heroic deeds of Voroshilov's and Budyenny's cavalrymen, who defeated the interventionist armies and drove them out of the young Soviet Republic.

Song of Return

Written by an Austrian refugee from Nazi oppression

It expresses the determination of anti-Nazi refugees dispersed throughout the world to unite in the common struggle and to return to their countries. The song ends with the chorus:

"We'll come again though and we'll smash to pieces
Who trod on the truth and the light,
We'll come again though and sing our old songs
Of homeland, of freedom, of right."

PICTURE 108
Young Austrians demonstrating their readiness to participate in the conflict, in a march to the City Centre. c. 1940.

PICTURE 109
Andre Drucker, today a celebrated author, painter and owner of several Viennese-type coffee bars in the city, at the keyboard in Islington Methodist Church Hall, St. Martin's Street, 30th September 1939.
He says: "I had the unusual experience of accompanying a choir of German-speaking Czechs through 'Where is my Home?' a Czech song, the words of which they did not understand."
Mr. Drucker was the Cultural Organiser of the Free Austrian Movement.

PICTURE 110
Theodor Teisen (seen with his national flag), a leading industrial furnace engineer from Kings Norton, concerned with the manufacture of vital war products. He later became the Danish Consul but during the war was a founder member of the Association of Free Danes, an organisation representing the Danish spirit in England during the German occupation. Some of the members are pictured below. PICTURE 111, His son Knud is the present Danish Consul in Birmingham.

PICTURE 112

In JUGOSLAVIA *then . . .*

In ENGLAND *now*

When the peasants of Jugoslavia were still free and their only enemy was the hard soil, a favourite feast dish was Raznjici (pork chops and onions grilled on skewers). But their daily dish often consisted of potatoes — *but* potatoes! The other day a number of Jugoslavian cooks were demonstrating potato cookery in London. Cheese Gibanica is one of the potato main-dishes they made. Here is the recipe for you to try.

CHEESE GIBANICA
Pastry : 2 oz. flour, water, pinch of salt. Enough water to make a soft dough. Put dough in floured cloth. Leave to set for 1 hour. Roll out thinly, pull out till as thin as paper, leave to dry in warm room. *Filling :* Make a mixture of ½ lb. mashed potatoes, 1 teaspoonful dried egg, sugar to taste, a little milk, knob of fat. Cut pastry to fit tin. Put alternate layers of pastry and filling, sprinkling each layer of filling with grated cheese. Make the top layer of pastry. Bake in moderate oven for 30 minutes.

Potatoes
are part of the battle

THE BOMBS FALL

PICTURE 113
High Street looking towards the Bull Ring, 10th April 1941.

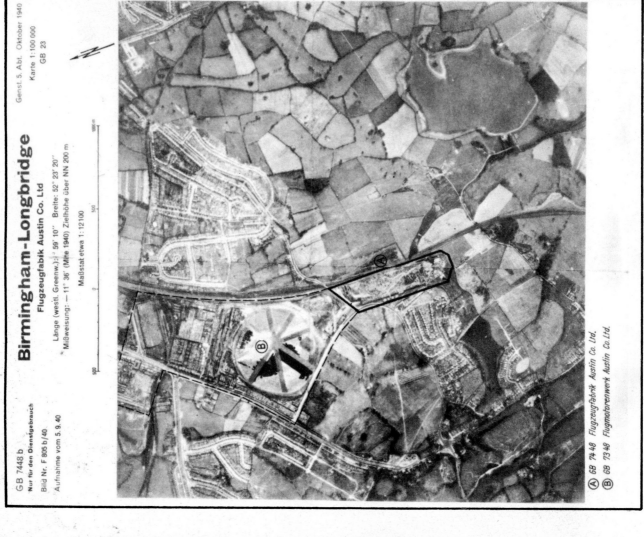

115

Birmingham-Longbridge

Flugzeugfabrik Austin Co. Ltd

Genst. 5. Abt. Oktober 1940
Karte 1:100 000
GB 23

GB 7448 b
Nur für den Dienstgebrauch
Bild Nr. F 805 b/40.
Aufnahme vom 5.9.40

Länge (westl. Greenw.): 1° 59′ 10″   Breite: 52° 23′ 20″
Mißweisung: — 11° 36′ (Mitte 1940) Zielhöhe über NN 200 m
Maßstab etwa 1:12100

Ⓐ GB 74 48 Flugzeugfabrik Austin Co. Ltd.
Ⓑ GB 73 48 Flugmotorenwerk Austin Co. Ltd.

114

Birmingham (Nord)

Saltley Railway Carriage and Waggon Works

1:8212 bc
468 L 35

23   72
B 6.39

PICTURE 116

Life gradually returning to normal in New Street, April 1941.

Bob Wilkes (Fireman, A.F.C. "B" Division): "There was a fire at the Co-op, High Street (to the left of the Times Building). I was wedged in a side window for a long while, unable to move because of the pressure of the jet. Afterwards the staff had a collection for me and what with the confusion and one thing and another, when I came out the appliance had returned to the station and I had to go back on the tram!"

Mrs. Dorothy Lloyd (daughter of Prime Minister Neville Chamberlain): "We lived near the city centre and were told that the safest place to shelter was under the stone staircase. Our cairn terrier Hamish was always the first to hear the whine of the falling devices — he was our own personal early bomb warning system."

116

PICTURE 117
A land mine wiped out the Malt Shovel on the island at the corner of John Bright Street and Hill Street on 19th/20th November 1940.
Top left hand corner shows the roof of New Street Station.
The square building in the centre of the photograph is The Grapes.

PICTURE 118
The Market Hall in the Bull Ring was gutted 25th/26th August 1940.
Anthony Beaumont-Dark, M.P.: "My father took me on the morning after and I remember seeing rabbits and guinea pigs being pursued around St. Martin's Churchyard. I think I first learned about business, during those days, from trading pieces of shrapnel with my school friends."

PICTURE 119
Steelhouse Lane, April 1941. The General Hospital can be seen at the bottom of the hill. The damage was caused by a high-explosive bomb which hit the Central Police Station, opposite, killing an inspector and six officers.

PICTURE 120
The Prince of Wales
Theatre, Broad Street,
victim of a direct hit,
9th April 1941.
Ironically, the theatre
had already been
scheduled by the city
fathers for demolition.

PICTURE 121

A view of the Theatre Royal in New Street, from Bennett's Hill, 11th April 1941. The show, at the time, was "He Didn't Want To Do It" starring Iris Hoey. The theatre, unlike the Empire in Hurst Street and the Prince of Wales in Broad Street, survived the bombings, but eventually closed its doors on 15th December 1956. Woolworth's now occupies the theatre site.

PICTURE 122

Workmen clearing up in front of Greys, Bull Street, November 1940.
Betty Hodgetts: "My boyfriend and I caught a No. 9 bus in Corporation Street, but because of the noise and overhead activity the driver stopped at Greys and we all had to get off. We stood there with people from other abandoned buses and then, after an hour, our driver alone decided, with us aboard, to make a dash for it. After a terrible journey we eventually got home. We later learned that, minutes after we left, a bomb landed right in front of the store and several people were killed."

123

PICTURE 123
Hockley Bus Depot devastated 22nd/23rd November 1940. 19 buses were burnt out, 4 partly burnt out and 88 damaged.

124

HIGHGATE ROAD GARAGE

PICTURE 124
Corner of Queen Street and Highgate Road, the morning of the 20th November 1940. 19 buses and 10 trams were damaged at this time.

Councillor Peter Hollingworth, Lord Mayor of Birmingham, 1982/3:

"We lived in Wentworth Road, Harborne and one night father called down, 'Come up, Peter, we've been hit.' I shot upstairs and found Dad, complete with stirrup pump and bucket, dealing with a burning incendiary. It had come through the ceiling, shattered the toilet and skidded under the bath. 'Get more water quickly,' said Dad, amidst the smoke, flame and horrible roaring noise. There were four taps in the bathroom and four in the conservatory, yet I was running up and down stairs getting water from the kitchen! It was just as well, as I noticed a glow under a bedroom door. A second bomb was burning through Dad's new dunlopillo mattress. We got both bombs out, but the mattress smouldered on the crazy paving for a week afterwards."

PICTURE 125 Colebrook Road, Greet, 30th January 1941.

PICTURE 127
Bridge St. West, Newtown, 30th July 1942.

PICTURE 128

John Taylor, actor (Peter Sellers' double in "Fu Manchu," Clouseau in "The Trail of the Pink Panther," etc.): "As a young boy on my way back from visiting my brother in St. Chad's Hospital I found a metal cylinder lying in the gutter in Portland Road, Edgbaston. I tied it with a piece of twine to the back of my bike and towed it to the police station. The officer in charge clipped my ear and told me it was an anti-personnel device and very dangerous. As I left they were tucking it under a sandbag."

The picture shows a typical such device, found by Charles Tipton.

129

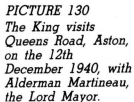

128

PICTURE 129
A bomb disposal officer tackles an unexploded device. Note the clock stopper attached to the bomb.

PICTURE 130
The King visits Queens Road, Aston, on the 12th December 1940, with Alderman Martineau, the Lord Mayor.

130

PICTURE 133 Mole Street/Stratford Road and St. Agatha's Church, Sparkbr

PICTURE 134 Bordesley Green.

PICTURE 131 Lily Road, South Yardley.

PICTURE 132 Oxford Road, Moseley.

PICTURE 136 Rear of Douglas Road, Handsworth.

PICTURE 138 Argyle Street, Nechells.

PICTURE 135 Katie. Road, Selly. Oak.

PICTURE 137 Cox's Screw Factory, Charles Henry Street, Highgate.

139

PICTURE 139 Medlicott Road, Sparkbrook, 27th August 1940　　*PICTURE 140 Nos 20-23 Balsall Heath Road.*

140

Do you know one of these?

Mr Secrecy Hush Hush

He's always got exclusive information — very private, very confidential. He doesn't want to spread it abroad but he doesn't mind whispering it to you — and others he meets. *Tell him to keep it to himself.*

Mr Knowall

He knows what the Germans are going to do and when they are going to do it. He knows where our ships are. He knows what the Bomber Command is up to. With his large talk he is playing the enemy's game. *Tell him so.*

Miss Leaky Mouth

She simply can't stop talking and since the weather went out as conversation she goes on like a leaky tap about the war. She doesn't know anything, but her chatter can do harm. *Tell her to talk about the neighbours.*

Miss Teacup Whisper

She is a relative of Mr. Secrecy Hush Hush and an equal danger. Everything she knows is so important it must be spoken in whispers all over the town. She's one of Hitler's allies. If she does not know that, *tell her (in a whisper).*

Mr Pride in Prophecy

Here is the marvellous fellow who knows how it is all going to turn out. Nobody else knows but he does. He's a fool and a public danger. *Give him a look* that tells him what you think of him.

Mr Glumpot

He is the gloomy brother who is always convinced that everything is going wrong and nothing can go right. He is so worried by the enemy's strength that he never thinks of ours. *Tell him to cheer up and shut up.*

Tell them all to
JOIN BRITAIN'S SILENT COLUMN

the great body of sensible men and women who have pledged themselves not to talk rumour and gossip and to stop others doing it.

ISSUED BY THE MINISTRY OF INFORMATION IN THE INTERESTS OF NATIONAL DEFENCE

141

PICTURE 142
German bomb disposal squad drill for a bomb in Warwick Road, Acocks Green.

PICTURE 143
German Prisoners of War search for suspected unexploded bombs in St. James' Churchyard, Handsworth.

ENTERTAINMENT AND SPORT

It would be wrong to think that life came to a halt. True, BBC Television had closed for the duration of the war, but few people in 1939 could afford a T.V. set anyway. However, 9 out of 10 homes had a radio set and the re-organised BBC Home Service was to produce some memorable programmes, including "ITMA," "Band Waggon," "Workers' Playtime," "Hi, Gang!" and, for the serious mind, "The Brains Trust." Two of the things that helped Brummies get through the war years were show business and sport.

Cinemas and theatres throughout the country closed due to the declaration of war and the fear of imminent bombing, but within a few weeks they had all re-opened.

In October 1939, the Football League was reorganised for the duration of the war, with 82 clubs taking part. Since many players were called up for military service it was not uncommon for scratch sides to take the field.

PICTURE 144
"I don't mind if I do, sir!"
Tommy Handley offers Jack Train (Col. Chinstrap) a light, if not a drink. Stars of "ITMA" take a well-earned break.

PICTURE 145
Richard "Stinker" Murdoch and Arthur Askey, stars of "Band Waggon," October 1942.

PICTURE 146
"The Aerials," BBC artists who formed a concert party to tour A.R.P. and A.F.S. sites. Many famous characters can be spotted, including pianist Harry Engleman, and actress Marjorie Westbury ("Steve" in "Paul Temple") and Dorothy Summers ("Mrs. Mop" in "ITMA"), December 1939.
This picture was provided by Barrie Edgar (3rd left) whose father Percy was Midland Region Director of the BBC in Broad Street. Barrie Edgar later became Senior T.V. Outside Broadcast Producer at Pebble Mill and his wife Joan was one of the first lady announcers.

147

PICTURE 147
The sound of music from young Pet Clark, with her soldier father Leslie, who was also her manager and scriptwriter.

PICTURE 148
Elsie and Doris Waters bring their "Gert and Daisy" characters to life, along with gossip about Bert, Wally, Old Mother Butler and all.

148

PICTURE 149
Vic Oliver, Bebe Daniels and Ben Lyon in "Hi, Gang!", a successful radio show and then a film, December 1941.

149

150

151

PICTURE 152
Groucho, Harpo, Douglas Dumbrille
and Chico Marx in "The Big Store,"
1941.

PICTURE 153   Moore Marriott, Will Hay and Graham Moffatt in
"Where's That Fire?", 1939.
Will Hay was a Fellow of the Royal Astronomical Society and, as a
sub-lieutenant in the RNVR, taught navigation to hundreds of cadets.

At the time of writing this programme note, it would seem that the widespread tension must inevitably affect the interest of our audiences and take their thought to graver matters. Strange as it may seem, however, the theatre, in larger sense, always survives epochs that may be termed catastrophic and in the past governments have deliberately insisted on its continuance as an outlet or escape for the community from the wear and tear of circumstances.

With this fact in mind, it may appear invidious to call your attention to the necessity of giving all possible support to our forthcoming programme, but in addition to what may prove hampering conditions under which our work will possibly be carried on, we are faced with an unusual and large outlay in the form of new electrical installation. The latter is a heavy charge on a theatre of small dimensions and the happiest and best way of meeting it is a spate of full houses.

Such hints are not new and you must forgive me for once more urging a continuance of the generous patronage which so many friends have extended to us in the past.

BARRY JACKSON.

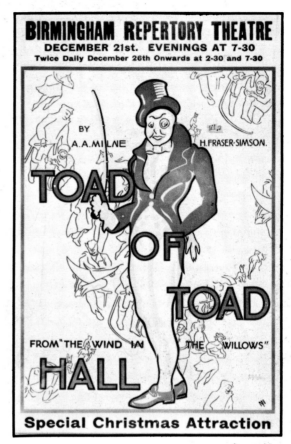

PICTURE 154 *Birmingham Repertory Theatre programme note, 2nd September 1939.*

PICTURE 156

A familiar scene to Birmingham theatregoers. The foyer of the Alexandra Theatre, with the audience about to enjoy a 1944 version of "Cinderella," starring Noele Gordon and George Doonan. Derek Salberg says in his engrossing book "My Love Affair With a Theatre" (reprinted here with his kind permission): "In order to impress Fred, my Sgt. Major, I took him to the theatre to show him round, but when I came to the top circle, it was manned by a newcomer who did not know me and would not let me in. I remonstrated mildly and finally, in desperation, said: 'Actually I am Derek Salberg,' to which he replied, 'I don't care if you're Winston Churchill — you're not coming in here without a ticket.'"

PICTURE 159
Dot Rawlins, dancing teacher: "I was a soubrette when this picture was taken in a munition works canteen in 1943, somewhere in Birmingham. Five shows per day were performed, including one at midnight. The shows were not only for the workers but for the firemen and security, especially at Christmas time, when the artistes would have dinner and tea at the factory. Costumes were a major headache during the war as you only had a few clothing coupons. My white dress was made of butter muslin. When doing troops shows we used to be picked up in the City Centre by army lorries with the windows blacked out. We were never told the destination and would travel whilst bombs were dropping. There was a Jewish comedian who used to appear dressed as Hitler. Picked up by the police, late one night, they searched his case and he had a lot of explaining to do."

PICTURE 157
Sandy Powell, Birmingham Hippodrome, 21st April 1941.

PICTURE 158
"Two Ton" Tessie O'Shea, Birmingham Hippodrome, 28th October 1940.

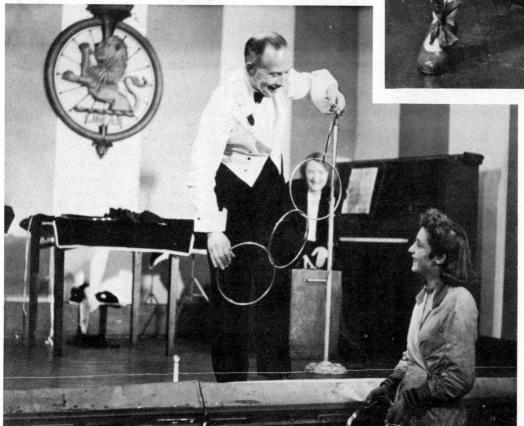

PICTURE 160

Workers' Playtime. Harold Hall (who later became Captain Entertainments Officer at the 6 Holding and Selection Centre, 21 Army Group, Belgium) performing the Chinese Linking Rings, a traditional effect that still confounds today, to an obviously enthralled Lucas worker.

PICTURE 161
Joe Loss (seen here with Glenn Miller and Vera Lynn) and his Orchestra were frequent visitors to the city. His wife Mildred says: "At that time I travelled with the band and was a 'mother' to them. On arrival in Birmingham one time, with an extremely hungry band, I discovered that most of the hotels, restaurants and shops were closed, due mainly to bomb damage. I scoured the city and finally found a shop where I must have bought up the entire stock. In fact, I remember returning to where the band were staying with bags that literally 'clanked' with tins of food."

PICTURE 162 Fred Newey, who still leads a band in Birmingham today, is seated at the piano at the King's Highway, Quinton, in October 1941. The vocalist is Hilda Hurst. He says: "Due to the petrol shortage, the band equipment was often carried to and from our gigs by a friendly greengrocer with a horse and cart."

DANCING, MUSIC, &C.

163

FRED Newey & his Orchestra vacant mid-wk. & Sats. incl. June 10 4 to 10-piece—53 World's End Avenue B'ham 32

165

City of Birmingham (Emergency) Orchestra

Musical Director – LESLIE HEWARD

Sixth Concert

in the

LARGE THEATRE, MIDLAND INSTITUTE

Saturday, December 2nd, 1939, at 2.30 p.m.

Programme :

OVERTURE, "Figaro" .. .. *Mozart*

Suite, "Le Bourgeois Gentilhomme" .. .. .. *Strauss*
  1. Overture to Act I   2. Minuet   3. The Fencing Master
  4. Entrance and Dance of the Tailors   5. The Minuet by Lully
  6. Courante   7. Scene of Cleonte (after Lully)   8. Prelude to Act II (Intermezzo)
  9. Dinner Music and Dance of the Kitchen Boy

Solo Pianoforte : ERIC HOPE

INTERVAL OF TEN MINUTES

SYMPHONY No. 7 in C .. .. *Schubert*
  Andante – Allegro ma non troppo   Andante con moto
  Scherzo and Trio (Allegro vivace)   Allegro vivace

Conducted by Victor Hely-Hutchinson

PRICE :
ONE PENNY

A. H. SHEPHARD, *Secretary,*
101, Corporation Street.

In the case of an Air Raid Warning the performance will continue. Patrons who wish to
leave are asked to do so as quietly as possible. The nearest way to the Basement Shelter
is by means of the Exit door adjoining the platform

PICTURE 164

The C.B.S.O. at their home in the Town Hall with conductor George
Weldon and leader Norris Stanley. The orchestra played in a variety of
local venues, including the West End. Stan Murphy, violinist: "Most of us
worked in munitions factories and George Weldon had to get permission
from our bosses for us to get time off to play."
Quite a few of the musicians also played in restaurants (Pattisons, Greys,
etc.) in trios and quartets.
The glorious organ, built in 1834 by William Hill, was the property of
the General Hospital until 1922. In 1932 Henry Willis & Sons Ltd. were
responsible for rebuilding it.

PICTURE 166
1st April 1940. Weigh-in at the Farcott Hotel, Rookery Road, Handsworth prior to the fight at the Tower Ballroom, Edgbaston.
Leamington's Dick Turpin on the left drew with the South African Eddie Maguire, but was beaten on points over 10 rounds on 20th May.
Please obey the air raid instructions.

PICTURE 7

The Warwickshire County Cricket Team prior to the outbreak of war. From left to right (back row) Ord, Wilmot, Hill, Dollery, Hollies, Shortland, Buckingham; (front row) Maher, Wyatt, Cranmer (capt.), Santall, Croom.

Tom Dollery: "We were playing at Lords, during the last week in August. The authorities asked us to get on with the game because war was imminent and London could be a major target. We finished the match a day early! On the way back the train was jam-packed with evacuees." From then on, the main cricketing events were festival weeks, the first of which was organised by the appropriately named Lt. Col. Scorer in 1942. "Rusty" Scorer also ran the Queensberry All-Services Club in Hurst Street.

PICTURE 168

An accidental fire gave the Birmingham City Football Club grandstand this "bomb damaged" look. The fans do not seem too dispirited, however.
Aston Villa allowed the Blues to use Villa Park for their home games in 1942/3.

PICTURE 169

Aston Villa F.C., winners of the wartime cup 1944/5, beating Blackpool 4-2 at Villa Park.
The players are, from left to right, (back row) Starling, Callaghan, Wakeman; (middle row) Iverson, Massey, Cummings, Parkes; (front row) Edwards, Potts, Broome, Houghton.
Harry Parkes, who supplied this picture, is today the owner of a thriving sports goods shop in Corporation Street.

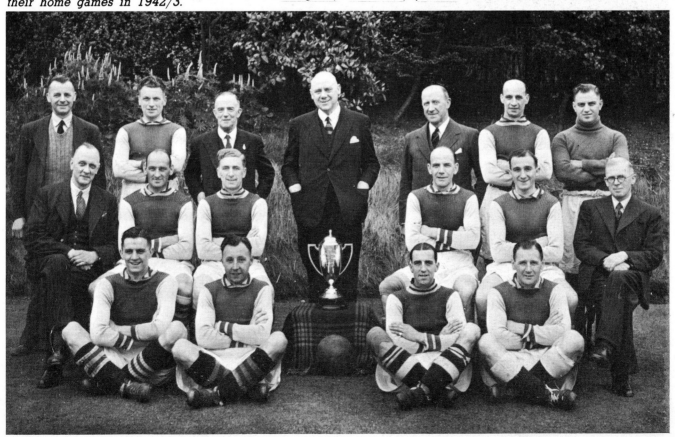

PICTURE 170

A mixed assortment of players — and jerseys! Camp Hill Old Edwardians Rugby Football Club, 1945.

PICTURE 171
Victor Barna.

172

GROUND FLOOR
Row 5

130

242

BRITISH RED CROSS SOCIETY
V.A.D. 52

IN AID OF B.R.C.S. & ST. JOHN PRISONERS' OF WAR FUND

A GRAND

Exhibition of Table Tennis

BY

WORLD FAMOUS CHAMPIONS

V. BARNA (Five times World Champion)

A. A. HAYDON (England Captain)   A. BROOK (English International)

A. SADLER (Welsh Captain)   T. LISLE (Welsh International)

TUESDAY, 21st DEC., 1943
BIRMINGHAM TOWN HALL

ADMISSION
3/6
(Reserved)

at 7-0 p.m.
●
Registered under the War Charities Act, 1940

Doors open 6-30 p.m.
M.C. : S. A. CARVER

AID FOR PRISONERS OF WAR

Many Birmingham ex-P.O.W.s have expressed gratitude for the parcels they received from the Red Cross collection centre at Grange Depot, Solihull. Again, this is used as a representative example.

PICTURE 173

PICTURE 174

The Birmingham Mail

N° 21,116

TUESDAY, JUNE 6, 1944

ONE PENNY

6.30

"SECOND FRONT" OPENS WELL

TROOPS SECURE BEACH-HEADS AT TWO POINTS

SEA AND AIR-BORNE INVASION OF FRANCE

ARMADA OF 4,000 SHIPS CROSSES CHANNEL

OPERATIONS PROCEEDING "ACCORDING TO PLAN"

THE "SECOND FRONT" HAS OPENED WELL AND ALREADY NEWS HAS BEEN RECEIVED THAT BRITISH AND CANADIAN TROOPS HAVE SECURED AT LEAST TWO BEACH-HEADS AND ARE DIGGING IN.

THE ALLIED TROOPS BEGAN LANDING OPERATIONS BETWEEN 6 A.M. AND 8.15 A.M. ON THE COAST OF NORMANDY. SIMULTANEOUSLY AIR-BORNE TROOPS AND PARATROOPS LANDED WHILE THE SHIPS OF THE BRITISH AND U.S. NAVIES BOMBARDED IMPORTANT OBJECTIVES.

The first news of the landing from British and American sources came in "Communique No. 1" from Supreme H.Q., Allied Expeditionary Force, at 9.33 a.m. This said:—

Under the command of General Eisenhower, Allied naval forces, supported by strong air forces, began landing Allied armies this morning on the Northern coast of France.

General Montgomery is in charge of the Army group carrying out the assault. This Army group includes British, Canadian and U.S. forces.

Later in the day Mr. Churchill told the Commons that so far the commanders reported that everything was proceeding according to plan—" and what a plan," he added. "This vast operation is undoubtedly the most complicated and most difficult which has ever occurred.

"The landings on the beaches are going on at various points at the present time.

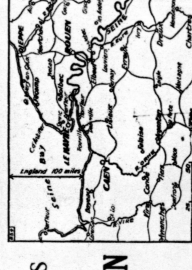

"I SAW THEM"

FIELDS WERE STREWN WITH PARACHUTES

TROOPS DROPPED THROUGH CLOUDS

Gladwin Hill, Associated Press war correspondent, representing the combined U.S. press, writes: Allied soldiers have landed in Northern France, and I saw them do it.

From the cockpit of a Marauder medium bomber I saw great naval and shore engagements getting under way.

A few miles inland I saw fields strewn with hundreds of parachutes, where Allied airborne forces had dropped. The fields were dotted too with aircraft, probably gliders, bearing the distinctive Allied invasion black and white zebra stripe, which was hurriedly slapped on the aircraft late yesterday.

The first signs of battle were flashes from the Channel below which, through the mist and naval smoke screen, gradually became distinguishable as gun detonations of warships shelling the coast.

The Channel was not "jammed with shipping," as might have been expected, but on every hand were forces of ships either battering the coast line or bringing up forces to take advantage of breaches.

William Wilson (Combined British press), who flew over one area in a bomber earlier writes: The Allied troops landed under a blanket of cloud 5,000 feet thick. In a flight up and down the French coast, we could see nothing, except clouds, the flash of heavy flak exploding and pale pinkish glow in the clouds in that area from the heavy bombardment below.

The airborne troops who passed over tactical bombers bases just before the bombers took off dropped to the ground through cloud.

Severe Flak

Over the Channel, closer to the British coast, the cloud broke and we could see escorted landing craft leaving long, twin wakes in the Channel behind them. A pilot from our base who missed his course on the return journey and flew over the coast reported a heavy attack on a long coastal strip. He said flares had been dropped, marking off an area. Both light and heavy flak were severe.

The bombers took off soon after midnight to begin the men landing in France by blocking the roads leading to the coast. Their job was to slow down Rommel's attempts to rush up reinforcements to meet the landings.

Bombers from our station were sent to attack bridges and road de-

FIRE OF BATTERIES ALMOST QUELLED

PREMIER'S STATEMENT IN COMMONS

"I have to announce to the House that during the night and the early hours of this morning the first of the series of landings in force upon the European Continent has taken place."

In these words the Premier announced the opening of the "Second Front" to the Commons.

"The liberating assault fell upon the coast of France," he went on. "An immense armada of upwards of 4,000 ships, together with several thousand smaller craft, crossed the Channel. Mass airborne landings have been successfully effected behind the enemy's lines. (Cheers.)

"Landings on the beaches are proceeding at various points at the present time. The fire of shore batteries has been largely quelled. The obstacles which were constructed in the sea have not proved so difficult as was apprehended. The Anglo-American Allies are sustained by about 11,000 first-line aircraft, which can be drawn upon as may be needed for the purposes of the battle.

"I cannot, of course, commit myself to any particular details as reports are coming in in rapid succession. So far the commanders who are engaged report that everything is proceeding according to plan—and what a plan! This vast plan is undoubtedly the most complicated and difficult that has ever occurred.

"It involves tides, wind, waves and visibility both from the air and sea standpoints, and the combined employment of land, air and sea forces in the highest degree of intimacy.

"There are already hopes that actual tactical surprise has been attained, owing to the care taken to furnish the enemy, with a succession of surprises during the course of the fighting.

"The battle which has now begun will grow constantly in scale and

Navy's Great Role

All Types of Allied Warships Engaged

Battleships, monitors and cruisers supported the Allied landings to bombard from long range German coastal defence batteries. Bombardments at shorter range against batteries and beach defence, were the assignment of destroyers and special close support vessels of the landing craft type.

The landing force will have to break through strong German defences, and to give weight to the attack, very large numbers of special craft are required.

Both the Royal and U.S. Navies supplied the landing craft. About half the smaller types of the British landing craft were manned and commanded by Royal Marines, and some of the infantry-carrying ships flew the Red Ensign of the British Merchant Navy.

For protection against air attack, the immense number of ships are all deterred by gunfire from shore batteries and attacking aircraft, they swept on, maintaining a steady course in tricky tides, keeping in perfect station to ensure that lines of dashings making the lane were dead straight. Ten thousands officers and men comprised the minesweeping force which cleared the channel and is still keeping it open.

U-Boat Protection

"Smokey Joes"

Included in the force were "Smokey Joes," coal-burning fleet sweepers which were sorting in the last war, and ships which, still on the secret list, were recently launched from the slipways of British and American yards. Several of the British flotillas in the operation were, in fact, built in America under "Lend-Lease." They went into action side by side with sister ships in the United States Navy.

The minesweepers were merely doing a routine job, doing it precisely as many other "100 per cent." sweeps had been done to clear enemy minefields round Britain's coasts, in the Mediterranean and elsewhere. Never before has any coast been so thickly strewn with mines. Undeterred by gunfire from shore batteries and attacking aircraft,

all equipped to deal with either moored or ground mines or both.

HOW ARMY MOVED

of events so that we may share such tribulations as may come to them and take joy in their achievements." (Cheers.)

Mr. Churchill: I will certainly endeavour, at any rate in the early part of this battle, to keep the House fully informed, and it may be that I shall ask their indulgence to trespass upon them before we rise to-day.

Mr. Gallacher: This is one of the most solemn moments in the life of Parliament, and it is certainly not a time for trying to make speeches.

Lowering his head and speaking with emotion, he added: "I would like to express my own feelings and, I think, the feelings of every member of this House, that our hearts and our thoughts are with those lads and the mothers who are at home." There was a murmur of sympa-

HOW THE NEWS WAS RECEIVED

"MAIL" RUSHED TO FACTORIES

SELLERS BESIEGED BY CROWDS

Life in the centre of Birmingham had barely had time to settle down to normality for the day before the momentous news was announced to the public officially through an early edition of the "Mail."

The news which thousands had been waiting so anxiously for was brought to them as speedily as humanly possible. War - time restrictions naturally curtailed the number of copies that could be printed, and these were rapidly absorbed by the public who swarmed around the few sellers who were able to obtain the papers in any quantity.

The first papers off the machines went away in a fast car to a large factory centre in Birmingham to break the news to the workers whose willing hands have toiled so long and constantly as their share of the effort that has made the Allied assault possible.

A "Mail" reporter stood in New Street to watch the public's reaction. There was no need to "shout the news from the house-tops." People sensed that something unusual was afoot. Without uttering a word a single seller was besieged by a crowd which at one time threatened to mob the man with the news under his arm. Wherever he moved, and

that was only a few feet at a time, the men, women, girls and boys followed him.

In rather less than 20 minutes he had disposed of 20 dozen papers. Coppers fell on the pavement and roadway all around him. He could not collect the money quickly enough but so helpful were the people receiving the news that none was lost. The pennies were picked up and thrust into the seller's pockets. "Is it worth buying?" asked one passer-by of the "Mail" reporter. The answer was: "Well, read it for yourself. I think you'll agree that it is."

"They are out early to-day, aren't they," commented another bystander. "The invasion's on; that's the reason," and away went the curious one to buy a paper for himself. As he read the striking headlines he turned to the "Mail" reporter and said "You're right."

R.A.F. Men Read It

Among the first Service men to read the news in the city were six pilots of the R.A.F. They greeted it in their usual calm manner, but one detected a decided glint in more than one of those half-a-dozen pairs of eyes. An American soldier sauntered across to see what all the fuss was about. When he read the news his sole comment was "That's a relief. We should be home by Christmas now."

Two Netherlands officers were quite unable at first to grasp the situation, but a young girl who had hung to the seller like a limpet explained it to them. Their reply was a ringing exchange of handshakes.

And yet another sidelight to the occasion was the attitude of a business man who, after scanning the front page — the only page that mattered remarked: "This will be very valuable one of these days."

For the lunch edition of the "Mail" people formed a long queue which had to be controlled by policemen at the junction of Cannon Street and New Street.

HE'S FOR IT!

PICTURE 178

On 6th June 1944, Britain awoke to the news of allied landings on the beaches of Normandy. The long-awaited Second Front had begun. The photograph shows people flocking to buy the 1 o'clock Mail in Cannon Street, for the first detailed news of the invasion. Within 100 days, over 2 million men, nearly half a million vehicles and 4¼ million tons of equipment were landed in France.

178

VICTORY

Starting at mid-afternoon on Sunday, 13th May, a victory parade consisting of 16,000 representatives of the military forces and some 40 civilian organisations proceeded round New Street, Corporation Street, Bull Street and Colmore Row, where the Lord Mayor took the salute outside the Council House. Vehicles were included in the procession, such as Y.M.C.A. mobile canteens and British Restaurant service vehicles.

The 100,000 or so spectators were packed so deeply that most of them could not see properly. Girls sat on youths' shoulders and women held up mirrors from their handbags to see a reflection of the parade. To obtain a vantage point youngsters climbed the trees in St. Philip's churchyard. Others sat on top of belisha beacons. Scaffolding at the corner of New Street was crammed with sightseers, some of whom stood on narrow planks eighty feet above ground. On Saturday, 29th September, Air-Marshal Sir Richard Peck, Assistant Chief of Air Ministry Staff, took the salute at the VJ (Victory over Japan) parade of 9,000 people. This started the city's Thanksgiving Savings Week aimed at boosting National Savings in order to help restore the economy. The target was £12,000,000 but the sum raised was actually £15,330,142!

PICTURE 179
Tuesday 8th May 1945. At 3 p.m. the Prime Minister, Winston Churchill, broadcasts to the world that the war with Germany has been won.

PICTURE 181 Wrens.

PICTURE 182 Spot that relative!

PICTURE 183
American Women's Army Corps.

PICTURE 187
Men of the 8th Punjab Pipe
Band lead detachments of
Indian and Ghurkha troops
as the parade enters New
Street from Victoria Square.

Members of the 8th Punjab
Pipe Band meet their public.
Note the happy trusting faces
of the little boys meeting,
for the first time, warriors
from a far-off land.

The Victory tram and bus.
Tom Hayes: "As Personnel
Manager of the Traffic
Division I travelled in the
tram over several routes
between 9th-15th May 1945.
Everywhere we were greeted
by cheering crowds who
were delighted to see such
an illuminated spectacle,
after the drabness of the
previous years."

THE KING'S EXAMPLE

SHARED DANGERS AND TRIALS OF PEOPLE

ADDRESSES FROM LORDS AND COMMONS

Addresses to the King and Queen are to be moved in the House of Commons and House of Lords on Tuesday. In the Lords' Address, to be moved by Lord Woolton, united and deeply felt congratulations are expressed on the cessation of hostilities in Europe.

Your Majesty and her Majesty the Queen, the Address goes on, have throughout the war shared with your people at home the trials and dangers through which they have had to pass. We cannot sufficiently express our admiration for the way in which you and the Queen have set an example at every stage of the struggle.

"You have been unwearied in encouraging your fighting forces, in showing your interest in the labours of war workers at home, in visiting the wounded, in comforting the bereaved, and in going among those who have lost their homes through enemy destruction.

"Your Majesty's forces and the combined determination of all your peoples have delivered Europe from its threatened bondage and have vindicated the cause of freedom both for ourselves and for others.

"We beg leave to assure your Majesty that our rejoicings in the victory won in Europe do not blunt the edge of our resolve to support in full measure the continuing war against Japan.

"Lastly, we venture to express to your Majesty our most earnest hope that your reign may long continue in conditions of peace at home and abroad, that progress along the British way of life may be happily achieved amongst us, and that aggression may be ended throughout the world."

The Commons Address

The Commons address which will be moved by Mr. Churchill, was in similar terms.

"We rejoice with your Majesty," it said, "in the deliverance brought both to this nation and to the enslaved peoples of Europe by the success of your Majesty's forces fighting in comradeship with those of your Majesty's allies.

"We would wish to express the deep feeling which exists throughout the whole country that your Majesty and your gracious consort have, from the beginning, contributed in a wonderful manner to the courage and constancy of the people by your inspiring example, by the extreme personal exertions you have made year after year, by your willingness to share all their trials, and your constant sympathy with them in the losses which they have endured."

Nuptial Trams

Returning home to Birmingham after several years' service abroad, a young Birmingham fighting man decided to get married. But this was to be no ordinary war-time marriage; he had lots of friends, and he was determined to have a "real slap-up" reception after the wedding. The major difficulty was that of transporting his 100 guests from the church. Taxis and cars were out of the question. Someone had a brainwave and suggested buses, but the Birmingham Transport Department shook its head sadly. Then another brainwave: Could he possibly have a tramcar? Of course, he could have a couple if he liked; but were the church and the "reception" on a tram route?

This unconquerable bridegroom saw to it that they were: Aston Old Church and a large Perry Barr inn teamed up. He and his bride and his scores of guests had two trams as wedding coaches—and, for once, on two Birmingham trams there was no strap-hanging.

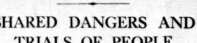

Flt.-Lieut. William Whitehouse, of Sparkhill, Birmingham, who received the D.F.C. at a recent investiture, is here seen outside Buckingham Palace with his mother, father, sister and aunt.

BELSEN CAMP

BIRMINGHAM WOMEN ON RELIEF WORK

HELPING RELEASED PRISONERS

Elisabeth Clarkson, formerly psychiatric social worker at the Birmingham Child Guidance Clinic, is helping released prisoners at Belsen concentration camp.

She is a member of a Friends' Relief Service team that left England in March, and after a brief period of relief work in Belgium, was sent to Belsen soon after its capture.

Over 10,000 prisoners who were seriously ill have been evacuated; half of them are not expected to survive. The nurses and doctors are attending to the less serious cases.

The Quaker men relief workers are inside the camp, engaged in sanitation, food supply and ambulance work.

The women members of the team are all working in the hospital. Miss Clarkson is working in a canteen. Another member of the team, Mrs. Kathleen Broughton, formerly cookery demonstrator for a Birmingham firm, is in charge of the catering at the hospital. Five hundred German "Wrens" are expected to help in nursing duties.

The leader of the Quaker team has set Hungarian women in the camp to making nightgowns for women patients and has collected urgently needed equipment and clothing from the abandoned houses of the S.S. officers and the Wehrmacht.

ELECTION RUMOURS

CONFLICTING ADVICE FOR MR. CHURCHILL

Mr. Churchill is considering when he ought to dissolve Parliament and have a General Election. He is being beckoned in two different directions by Unionist advisers, writes a Lobby correspondent.

One persuasive group is saying, "You must have a snap election at the end of June or the beginning of July. That is the surest way of securing a Unionist victory, because your own personal popularity in the country will then be at its height."

The other Unionist voice takes the opposite view. "Our party organisations in the constituencies are not yet prepared, as was proved at Chelmsford," says this voice.

"In any case a snap election could be turned against us as political sharp practice after the long team work of the Coalition. The proper election time is October or November.

"Why not continue the present Government until the war with Japan is won—or have a Unionist caretaker Government that would pass one or two valuable reconstruction measures as a sample of what Unionists would do if returned?"

Now a third consideration has sprung up which may influence Mr. Churchill's mind much more than any of these.

The election registers are simply not ready. Chaos at some of the polling booths might occur under the present state of things.

Some of the enormous reconstruction difficulties now that war workers and others are going home and big populations are shifting will be brought out in Wednesday's debate on resettlement.

REST OF THE NEWS

MORE DUTCH CHILDREN COMING TO BRITAIN

Another 18,000 Dutch children will shortly come to Br'tain for rest and rehabilitation, reported Dutch radio to-day.

"Picture of the Week."—The picture to be exhibited in Birmingham Art Gallery on Monday as the "Picture of the Week" will be a Welsh landscape, "Roman Amphitheatre near Festiniog," by John Piper.

Hindu Pilgrims' Disaster.—Thirty-one Hindu pilgrims, on their way to the holy shrine at Badrinath, were killed when a bus plunged hundreds of feet down a mountain precipice. The passengers also included several Bengal ladies.

Canada's War Casualties.—Canadian Army, Navy and Air casualties up to May 7 were 102,875. This includes 37,206 dead and 3,769 missing. In the first Great War Canadian casualties were 190,692, including 62,617 dead.

Vegetables & Flowers "Special."—Two thousand boxes of lettuce, watercress and French beans with quantities of roses, carnations, sweet peas and pinions arrived by G.W.R. from the West Country to-day for London markets.

Ida Lupino Granted Divorce.—Ida Lupino, British-born film actress and daughter of the late Stanley Lupino, was yesterday granted a divorce from Louis Hayward, the South African actor, states a Hollywood message.

German Soldiers' Request Refused.—Swiss radio states that about 4,000 German soldiers landed at different places on the Swedish coast and asked to be interned. The Swedish authorities refused their request and ordered them to leave Swedish territory within 48 hours.

Halesowen Child's Injuries.—Irene Joan Barratt (aged 3), of 84, Stourbridge Road, Halesowen, was detained in the Birmingham Accident Hospital to-day suffering from a fractured skull and other injuries received when knocked down by a motor lorry in High Street, Halesowen.

No "Fairy Land of Plenty."—Ontario's Liberal leader, Mr. M. F. Hepburn, criticising a pamphlet believed to come from London, said it was likely to start mass immigration by representing Ontario as a "fairy land of plenty," and would be unfair to English people proposing to come to Ontario.

This Week's Double

Evidently inspired by the magnificent news, a Rhode Island Red hen belonging to Mr. Leslie Richardson, of 32, Woodgreen Road, Quinton, laid an egg equal in size to the events of Tuesday. It was about three times the weight and size of an average hen egg, and was of curious structure. Two eggs were contained in the one shell, one having an inner shell of its own, and the other only the yolk and white—symbolical of V E-Day and V+1.

ROBIN GOODFELLOW.

CATHEDRAL SERVICE RELAY

At 6.30 to-morrow evening, a thanksgiving service at Birmingham Cathedral will be relayed to the churchyard outside, at which an orchestra will accompany the singing of hymns.

STREET PARTIES

At 2.41 a.m. on Monday, 7th May 1945 Germany surrendered unconditionally, with hostilities to end at one minute past midnight of Tuesday, which was declared Victory in Europe day, a public holiday extending to Wednesday. VE day saw streets everywhere burst miraculously into a pageant of colour with bunting and flags, setting the scene for parties for the children and uninhibited merrymaking all round. Bonfires were fuelled with redundant black-out material and effigies of Nazi leaders.

Thousands made for Victoria Square, but were disappointed to miss Churchill's speech, as loudspeakers had not yet been installed. The Lord Mayor, Alderman Wiggins-Davies, placed his own radio at an open window of his parlour, but few could hear. In the evening, however, at least 30,000 in the Victoria Square area heard the King's speech, at the end of which they sang "There'll always be an England."

Impromptu singing and dancing continued till morning, and people thronged the city centre for more revelry on this second day, on which innumerable street parties were again enjoyed. The Lord Mayor and Lady Mayoress covered 90 miles touring these parties on the Tuesday and 140 on the Wednesday.

At midnight on Tuesday 14th August came the announcement of the end of the war against Japan, and soon afterwards more than 12,000 people had converged on the city centre to revel in the light of a bonfire. Two days of celebration followed the same pattern as for VE.

PICTURE 192 The sun shining brightly on the residents of Stoneleigh Road, Perry Barr.

PICTURE 191 Tea up! Dimsdale Road, Northfield.

PICTURE 193

The folk of Sylvia Avenue, King's Heath, immortalised by the Honourable Alderman George Evans.

106

PICTURE 194

Waiting for the feast to start. Neighbours
of Dovedale Road, Perry Common,
remembered by Mrs. Flora Jones who, at
the age of 90, still lives in the same house.

PICTURE 195

Considering the scarcity of materials, this
group from Ditton Grove, West Heath,
certainly put on a spectacular Fancy Dress
display.

195

THE WAR IS OVER

196

PICTURE 196
And still the men were returning to Birmingham. Here, on 11th February 1946, magician Lou E. Flynn entertains some of the 350 wounded soldier guests at a party given by the Wholesale and Retail Fruit Trade at the British Restaurant in Cambridge Street.

Lou, now in his eighties, is still an active member of the British Magical Society.

PICTURE 197
First P.O.W.s repatriated from Germany enjoy a meal at the Grand Hotel.

197

PICTURE 198
The Lord Mayor, Alderman W. T. Wiggins-Davis, and civic and church dignitaries arrive for the Thanksgiving Service at the Hall of Memory, Suffolk Street, 24th May 1945. Edmund Street is on the right

PICTURE 199
The Thanksgiving
Service in progress

"For King and Country — for Dear Life — for Freedom of Mankind."

JOSEPH LUCAS LTD.

This is to certify that

WAS EMPLOYED AT THE
Factory

IN THE PRODUCTION OF VITAL WAR
WEAPONS & EQUIPMENT
FOR THE
ROYAL NAVY · THE ARMY · THE R·A·F
& SO PLAYED A FULL PART IN HELPING
OUR ARMED FORCES TO VICTORY

*This is a typical certificate
issued by Birmingham firms
at the end of the war.*

200

111

FRONT COVER: Victory tram.

TITLE PAGE: What may have been the world's largest poster, and certainly the largest in Britain, was erected on Birmingham's Town Hall for Warship Week.

The poster made an inspiring appeal and depicted the Navy's capital ships going into action with the phantom of Nelson rising from the sea, and two banners 50ft. long bearing Nelson's famous flag signal hung each side.

The poster was 150ft. long by 50ft. deep and was 7,500 sq. ft. in area, which gives some idea of its vast size. Nelson's head alone was 40ft. high. Besides other things 5,000ft. of timber and 50 gallons of paint in 25 different colours went to make it. The poster was painted in panels, each 12ft. x 8ft. and so enthusiastic were the artists in their task for the national effort that they used every glimmer of daylight and finished the job in a week. (The poster was designed and painted by the Advertising Staff of Joseph Lucas Ltd.).

BACK COVER—Top: The good ship "Ladywood" takes to the waters of the Birmingham Canal in August 1940.

Centre: Damaged house at the corner of Beaks Hill Road and Rednal Road, Kings Norton, 28th July 1942.

Bottom: Four evacuees.

ACKNOWLEDGEMENTS

(For providing anecdotes, memories, photographs, encouragement and numerous other favours) The Birmingham Post & Mail Staff; Birmingham Reference Library, Local Studies Dept.; Derek Salberg; George Bartram; Robert Holmes; Joe and Mildred Loss; Dorothy Lloyd; Austin Rover, Longbridge; Tom Dollery; Leslie Deakins; Warwickshire C.C.C.; Peter Hollingworth; Anthony Beaumont-Dark; Joyce Cadbury; Andre Drucker; Fred Newey; John Taylor; Maurice Price; John Clarke; Bob Wilkes; Dave Carpenter; Stan Murphy; William O. Alexander; Ruby Massa; Lily Moody; Pat Hatfield; Colin and Connie Wootton; Boys' Brigade; C.B.S.O.; Cadbury/Schweppes Ltd.; Birmingham Repertory Theatre; Lucas Industries PLC; Aston Villa F.C., PLC; Birmingham City F.C., PLC; Harry Parkes; George Auster; Arthur Camwell; Stan Jefferson; Joyce Chatwin; Joe Russell; Norman Power; Douglas Jones; St. John's House, Warwick; Bovington Tank Museum; Bruce Normansell; John Garrad; Jock Kilgour; George Evans; Margo Millington; Barrie and Joan Edgar; B.B.C.; Knud and Inge Teisen; Bud Abbott; Equity; Dot Rawlins; British Magical Society; Harold Hall; Lou E. Flynn; West Midlands Police; Ronald Mackenzie; Lewis's; Flora Jones; Birmingham Jewish Recorder; Norman Gibbons; West Midlands Passenger Transport Executive; Betty Hodgetts; Tom Hayes; West Midlands Branch of the Red Cross; Salvation Army; Leslie Hill; Record Centre; Frank Manley; John Croucher; Saltley School; Syd Jackson; National Bus Company; Edgbaston Golf Club; Girl Guides' Association; W.R.V.S.; Thorn EMI Gas Appliances Ltd.; St. Benedict's Road School; Anthony Webber; Aerospace Museum, RAF Cosford.